SECOND EDITION

CREATIVITY in the PRIMARY CLASSROOM

Juliet Desailly

Los Angeles | London | New Delhi
Singapore | Washington DC

Los Angeles | London | New Delhi
Singapore | Washington DC

SAGE Publications Ltd
1 Oliver's Yard
55 City Road
London EC1Y 1SP

SAGE Publications Inc.
2455 Teller Road
Thousand Oaks, California 91320

SAGE Publications India Pvt Ltd
B 1/I 1 Mohan Cooperative Industrial Area
Mathura Road
New Delhi 110 044

SAGE Publications Asia-Pacific Pte Ltd
3 Church Street
#10-04 Samsung Hub
Singapore 049483

Commissioning editor: James Clark
Assistant editor: Rachael Plant
Production editor: Nicola Marshall
Copyeditor: Audrey Scriven
Indexer: Author
Marketing executive: Dilhara Attygalle
Cover design: Naomi Robinson
Typeset by: C&M Digitals (P) Ltd, Chennai, India
Printed in Great Britain by Henry Ling Limited
at The Dorset Press, Dorchester, DT1 1HD

© Juliet Desailly 2015

First edition published 2012

This second edition published 2015

Library of Congress Control Number: 2015932286

British Library Cataloguing in Publication data

A catalogue record for this book is available from
the British Library

MIX
Paper from
responsible sources
FSC
www.fsc.org   FSC™ C013985

ISBN 978-1-4739-1255-7
ISBN 978-1-4739-1256-4 (pbk)

At SAGE we take sustainability seriously. Most of our products are printed in the UK using FSC papers and boards.
When we print overseas we ensure sustainable papers are used as measured by the Egmont grading system.
We undertake an annual audit to monitor our sustainability.

CREATIVITY in the
PRIMARY CLASSROOM

Llyfrgelloedd Caerdydd
www.caerdydd.gov.uk/llyfrgelloedd
Cardiff Libraries
www.cardiff.gov.uk/libraries

SAGE was founded in 1965 by Sara Miller McCune to support the dissemination of usable knowledge by publishing innovative and high-quality research and teaching content. Today, we publish more than 850 journals, including those of more than 300 learned societies, more than 800 new books per year, and a growing range of library products including archives, data, case studies, reports, and video. SAGE remains majority-owned by our founder, and after Sara's lifetime will become owned by a charitable trust that secures our continued independence.

Los Angeles | London | New Delhi | Singapore | Washington DC

CONTENTS

ABOUT THE AUTHOR

Juliet Desailly has worked in Education for over thirty years. Having trained originally as a specialist drama teacher and then working in Theatre-in-Education, when she became a primary teacher she brought a range of different teaching and learning methods to her work.

Juliet worked in Inner London primary schools for over twenty years, refining and adapting the primary curriculum to suit the children she taught – integrating social and emotional skills within the curriculum, emphasising the children's identity and culture, and raising self-esteem by providing an inclusive curriculum for all learners.

As well as her teaching and work in Theatre-in-Education Juliet has been a Humanities adviser and a deputy head teacher. After seven years as a lecturer at the Institute of Education on the Primary PGCE course, she now works as a consultant in creativity and curriculum planning.

Juliet has written a large amount of educational material, including two series of *Infant History* for BBC Radio and materials for the Education Department's Social and Emotional Aspects of Learning (SEAL) resource. Her first children's book, *Ma'at's Feather*, a story set in Ancient Egypt, and a set of accompanying cross-curricular lesson ideas, were published in 2008, and Juliet travels the country offering talks and practical workshops to primary school classes based on the book.

ACKNOWLEDGEMENTS

It has been an interesting task updating this second edition. So much has changed in schools in recent years and yet, at the time of writing, there seems to be a sense of primary schools holding their breath and waiting to see what will happen next. I sincerely hope that what does happen is that teachers can look towards the future confident that exploring and extending their own and their pupils' creativity will improve that future for everyone.

Yet again I need to acknowledge the enormous help, encouragement and support of my family. More thanks than I can say are due to my husband, Alan, and daughters, Rossy and Nancy, for their patience when I was stressed, for reading and commenting wisely on the manuscript, for their interest and enthusiasm, and not least for their huge moral support.

Primary school teachers are by nature borrowers and adaptors of ideas and information. I have spent over thirty years in the company of other teachers and students, listening, watching, discussing and always picking up ideas to try to adapt to my own uses. As such, I cannot possibly remember or give credit individually to all those amazing teachers young and old whose creativity and inventiveness have contributed to the ideas in this book. All I can say is a blanket 'thank you' to every child I have taught, every student I have observed, and every colleague I have worked with for all I have gained from you. I hope I have passed it on usefully in my turn. To John Cook and Jill Bonner, the head teachers who particularly fostered and valued my creativity as a teacher, many thanks.

All my former colleagues at the Institute of Education were generous with their interest and support. Particular thanks go to Anne Robertson, the Primary PGCE course leader, for giving her time so generously, particularly on the ideas for the Further Study sections.

Finally, many thanks to James Clark, Rachael Plant and all the staff at SAGE Publications for their patience, advice and hard work in the production of this book.

SAGE would like to thank the following reviewers, whose comments helped to shape this new edition:

Emese Hall, University of Exeter
Karan Vickers-Hulse, University of the West of England
Pauline Palmer, Manchester Metropolitan University
Yvonne Rennalls, Birmingham City University

TEACHERS' STANDARDS REFERENCE TABLE

Teachers' Standards		Where this book helps you meet these standards
A teacher must:		
1	**Set high expectations which inspire, motivate and challenge pupils**	
1a	establish a safe and stimulating environment for pupils, rooted in mutual respect	Chapter 4
1b	set goals that stretch and challenge pupils of all backgrounds, abilities and dispositions	Chapters 4, 7
1c	demonstrate consistently the positive attitudes, values and behaviour which are expected of pupils	Chapters 4, 5, 8
2	**Promote good progress and outcomes by pupils**	
2a	be accountable for pupils' attainment, progress and outcomes	
2b	be aware of pupils' capabilities and their prior knowledge, and plan teaching to build on these	Chapter 7

(Continued)

2c	guide pupils to reflect on the progress they have made and their emerging needs	Chapters 3, 4
2d	demonstrate knowledge and understanding of how pupils learn and how this impacts on teaching	By taking part in the individual, group and further study activities
2e	encourage pupils to take a responsible and conscientious attitude to their own work and study	Chapters 3, 4
3	**Demonstrate good subject and curriculum knowledge**	
3a	have a secure knowledge of the relevant subject(s) and curriculum areas, foster and maintain pupils' interest in the subject, and address misunderstandings	
3b	demonstrate a critical understanding of developments in the subject and curriculum areas, and promote the value of scholarship	Chapters 1, 2, 5
3c	demonstrate an understanding of and take responsibility for promoting high standards of literacy, articulacy and the correct use of standard English, whatever the teacher's specialist subject	
3d	if teaching early reading, demonstrate a clear understanding of systematic synthetic phonics	
3e	if teaching early mathematics, demonstrate a clear understanding of appropriate teaching strategies	
4	**Plan and teach well structured lessons**	
4a	impart knowledge and develop understanding through effective use of lesson time	Chapter 3
4b	promote a love of learning and children's intellectual curiosity	Chapter 5
4c	set homework and plan other out-of-class activities to consolidate and extend the knowledge and understanding pupils have acquired	
4d	reflect systematically on the effectiveness of lessons and approaches to teaching	Chapter 7
4e	contribute to the design and provision of an engaging curriculum within the relevant subject area(s)	Chapters 8, 9

5	**Adapt teaching to respond to the strengths and needs of all pupils**	
5a	know when and how to differentiate appropriately, using approaches which enable pupils to be taught effectively	Chapters 3, 6
5b	have a secure understanding of how a range of factors can inhibit pupils' ability to learn, and how best to overcome these	Chapter 4
5c	demonstrate an awareness of the physical, social and intellectual development of children, and know how to adapt teaching to support pupils' education at different stages of development	Chapter 4
5d	have a clear understanding of the needs of all pupils, including those with special educational needs; those of high ability; those with English as an additional language; those with disabilities; and be able to use and evaluate distinctive teaching approaches to engage and support them	Chapters 4, 6
6	**Make accurate and productive use of assessment**	
6a	know and understand how to assess the relevant subject and curriculum areas, including statutory assessment requirements	Chapter 7
6b	make use of formative and summative assessment to secure pupils' progress	Chapter 7
6c	use relevant data to monitor progress, set targets, and plan subsequent lessons	
6d	give pupils regular feedback, both orally and through accurate marking, and encourage pupils to respond to the feedback	Chapter 7
7	**Manage behaviour effectively to ensure a good and safe learning environment**	
7a	have clear rules and routines for behaviour in classrooms, and take responsibility for promoting good and courteous behaviour both in classrooms and around the school, in accordance with the school's behaviour policy	Chapter 4
7b	have high expectations of behaviour, and establish a framework for discipline with a range of strategies, using praise, sanctions and rewards consistently and fairly	Chapter 6

(Continued)

(Continued)

7c	manage classes effectively, using approaches which are appropriate to pupils' needs in order to involve and motivate them	Chapters 3, 4
7d	maintain good relationships with pupils, exercise appropriate authority, and act decisively when necessary	
8	**Fulfil wider professional responsibilities**	
8a	make a positive contribution to the wider life and ethos of the school	Chapter 8
8b	develop effective professional relationships with colleagues, knowing how and when to draw on advice and specialist support	
8c	deploy support staff effectively	
8d	take responsibility for improving teaching through appropriate professional development, responding to advice and feedback from colleagues	By taking part in the individual, group and further study activities
8e	communicate effectively with parents with regard to pupils' achievements and well-being	

Source: DfE (2011)

SUBJECTS AND SKILLS REFERENCE TABLE

The classroom ideas and classroom examples boxes and case studies include practical teaching ideas, examples and lesson plans to use in the following subjects or skill sets:

Subject/skill	Relevant pages
Cross-curricular	105, 141–142, 143, 150–154
Design and technology	15, 50
Drama	155–160
English	86, 125, 132, 152, 155–158
Geography	125, 132, 155–158
History	30, 55, 107, 132, 139
Learning skills	15, 47, 50, 66, 68, 69, 73
Mathematics	116–118, 158–160
PSHE	63, 65, 87
Teaching skills	84
Thinking skills	51, 55, 86, 101

INTRODUCTION

What do we want a classroom in a primary school in the second decade of the twenty-first century to look like? Children sat in rows looking at the board? Children involved in investigations and experimentation? Children working silently and alone? Children debating enthusiastically in groups? Or perhaps all of these things at different times? And what do we mean by a 'classroom'? Could the learning be happening outside, in the community or a natural environment?

As teachers, we need to help prepare young people for life in a rapidly changing society where they can be innovative, responsive and fulfilled. We will need the ability to use methods of teaching and learning within a curriculum that will make that possible.

Many schools have been adapting what and how they teach and how the learning is organised to make it more holistic, more engaging, more personalised, and more creative. The White Paper that heralded the arrival of the new National Curriculum promised 'scope for teachers to inspire' and envisaged 'teachers taking greater control over what is taught in schools, innovating in how they teach and developing new approaches to learning' (DfE, 2010: 40). As the curriculum embeds there will be consequent opportunities and challenges for teachers to provide the best and most appropriate learning opportunities for the children they teach. The aims of the new National Curriculum state that it 'is just one element in the education of every child' and that it 'provides an outline of core knowledge around which teachers can develop exciting and stimulating lessons' (DfE, 2014: 6). In criticising the previous National Curriculum for 'squeezing out room for innovation, creativity, deep learning and intellectual exploration' (DfE, 2010: 40) the White Paper implicitly supported these aspects. With less content and these assurances this is surely the time for teachers to take the opportunity to develop and practise teaching methods that will inspire young people and allow for deeper learning.

To strike a balance between all the constituent parts of both the National Curriculum and the broader curriculum, to find teaching methods that inspire and motivate young people to learn deeply and well will be a challenge for teachers joining the profession, and for more experienced teachers as well. They will have to be flexible and to learn new skills in the way they plan and teach, but it will also give the opportunity for teaching and learning that are exciting and fulfilling for children and teachers alike.

Defining creativity

Creativity has always proved hard to define, both in education and in its wider contexts. However, it has also been something that has been thought valuable and worth promoting. A search for 'benefits of creativity' on the internet will result in countless examples of business, psychology, health, philosophy and education claiming the importance of encouraging creativity. The first aim of the 1999 National Curriculum (known as Curriculum 2000) states, '... the curriculum should enable pupils to think creatively and critically, to solve problems and to make a difference for the better. It should give them the opportunity to become creative, innovative, enterprising and capable of leadership to equip them for their future lives as workers and citizens' (DfEE/QCA, 1999). During the first decade of the twenty-first century there were several developments designed to foster and promote creativity, including a joint-department review called *Nurturing Creativity in Young People* (DCMS/ DfES, 2006) and the report and teachers' resources *Creativity: Find it, Promote it* (QCA, 2005).

Teachers have long been aware of the importance to children's learning of the spark of creativity in children's descriptions and art work: 'It's like a rainbow was caught and shining in his eye'. They see how children invent methods for problem solving or find patterns in data or images. They relish the enthusiasm and intense concentration children show when involved in exploring materials or mixing ingredients, but these moments of classroom magic have often seemed at odds with the drive to raise standards. The research and understanding of the benefits of creativity and creative learning are still often sidelined or ignored.

In the final report of the Cambridge Primary Review, which was published in 2010, the director of the review, Professor Robin Alexander, commented that in submissions to the review 'the words "creative" and "creativity" appeared ... more frequently than almost any others'. He continued that the words 'invariably were regarded positively. The words were also used somewhat loosely' (Alexander, 2010: 226). This 'loose' terminology sees the term 'creativity' used to describe arts subject areas, cross-curricular planning, working without preconceived outcomes, creative teaching, children's creativity ... and this list is not exclusive.

Mathilda Marie Joubert agrees that 'creativity is a very elusive concept to define, and even when defined, it is interpreted in a variety of different ways' (2001: 29), and argues that we do not have a shared language for creativity. Despite these difficulties, creativity returns again and again in both what schools and teachers want to provide for their pupils and what industry and successive governments want in the workforce.

Defining terms in education today is a matter of some significance; there have been countless debates as to what is meant by domains and subjects, knowledge and understanding, skills and concepts, to name but a few. The politicisation of education has led to the polarisation of viewpoints and various 'camps' have emerged. In the discourse, creativity has often been equated with progressivism or even 'sloppiness'.

However, educational theorists in recent years, working alongside psychologists and neuroscientists, have actually defined quite clearly where creativity sits within education and it is far from its connotations as lacking rigour or 'anything goes'. Joubert states, 'We have to reclaim the meaning of the word "creativity". Creativity should be rigorous, it is grounded in knowledge and skills and there should be a balance between freedom and control in all creative activities' (2001: 30). This is not to say that scholarly debates do not continue, but even if we are still not decided as to whether creativity is an 'intelligence' or a 'state of mind' (Lucas, 2001: 40), we are able to categorise creativity in education into its three distinct parts – teaching creatively, learning creatively and teaching to develop creativity – and to recognise the key elements, strengths and benefits of these three approaches and how to acquire and develop the knowledge and skills to use them appropriately in the classroom.

Effective teaching and learning

There is a strong argument (see Jeffrey and Craft, 2001) that creative teaching is actually 'effective teaching'. Amongst the 'noticeable characteristics' of outstanding student teachers in the Ofsted criteria published in 2008 are the following:

- '... take risks when trying to make teaching interesting, are able to deal with the unexpected';
- '... show innovative and creative thinking';
- '... have the ability to reflect critically and rigorously on their own practice to inform their professional development, and to take and evaluate appropriate actions'.

As will be seen from the subsequent chapters in this book, these are key elements of creativity themselves. Becoming a teacher who is able to teach creatively and encourage pupils to learn creatively and develop their own creativity is also to become a highly effective teacher.

Anna Craft also argues that 'in a constructivist frame, learning and creativity are close, if not identical' (Craft, 2005: 61) and that teaching for creativity is 'learner empowerment'. The (2010) Ofsted report, *Learning: Creative Approaches that Raise Standards*, focused on schools that used creative approaches to teaching and learning and their effectiveness in raising standards of education. The report was clear that effective creative teaching and learning were rigorous and well organised: 'Careful planning had ensured that the prescribed curriculum content for each subject was covered within a broad and flexible framework and key skills were developed. These examples were accompanied by better than average achievement and standards or a marked upward trend' (2010: 5). Ofsted reported that for 'schools in this survey with a wide ability range, a focus on creative learning was driven by the need to break down barriers to learning and improve achievement. In all cases, the survey found that this was effective' (2010: 15).

Benefits of creativity

Teaching creatively and to develop creativity brings many benefits to both teachers and learners. A creative teacher will challenge, engage and motivate pupils, placing learning within contexts that have relevance for the children they teach. A creative learner will be developing intellectual and academic skills that will last a lifetime. Being creative involves both generating new ideas and synthesising a variety of other peoples' ideas into a new understanding. It also involves reflection and evaluation as part of the process so that creative learners are constantly asking themselves questions as to the best way to proceed. Creativity involves finding patterns, researching, hypothesising and generalising. As well as being investigative and enquiring, a creative person will be reaching conclusions and able to argue 'I think this because ... '.

Much is made at the present time of comparing our educational 'performance' with that of other countries. It is interesting that in those that are hailed for their superior achievements, factors include being able 'to generalise and creatively use information based on their own investigations and modelling of complex problem situations' (OECD, quoted in a speech by Michael Gove, January 2011) and 'increasing the emphasis on deep understanding, the ability to apply knowledge to solving new problems and the ability to think creatively' (OECD, 2011). Creativity provides exactly this.

A creative learner will also be developing social and emotional skills. The need for persistence, determination and an understanding of delayed gratification is necessary for creative approaches, and teachers will need to help children develop these skills as they foster and enhance other skills that are necessary for working creatively. Although creativity can be a solitary way of working it is often at its most effective when working with others. Learning to work well in a group situation, listening, debating, working in a community of enquiry and being able to disagree, agree and move others' ideas forward in a constructive way, are all integral skills for working creatively.

Creativity can also involve expressing personally held views and opinions or sharing ideas in expressive media. As such, it involves a measure of self-confidence and the ability to be a risk taker.

About this book

Aims

Creativity in the Primary Classroom is designed to be of use and interest both to trainee teachers and to qualified teachers at any stage in their careers who want to understand better what creativity in the primary classroom looks like, its value, and how it can be achieved.

The book's intention is to be accessible and full of practical ideas to use in the classroom, based on and referencing key texts and research by experts in the area. It encourages a flexible approach to suit the very different needs of teachers with various experience and styles of teaching in a variety of different schools.

The text aims to reflect what creativity in a primary classroom can look like and the activities that teachers and children might be engaged in. As such, it includes examples and descriptions from classroom practice, ideas to use straightaway, and some longer case studies to show the theories in practical situations. Visualising what one would actually see, hear and do in a classroom situation can be extremely difficult. Hopefully, this book will demystify the subject and make practical solutions readily available.

Rather than being organised on a subject-by-subject basis this book examines creativity as a generic entity, and as such demonstrates how the key elements of creativity can be applied to any and every subject and across the curriculum as a whole. There is, however, some guidance in finding and using the elements of creativity in specific subjects.

Organisation and structure

The book is organised into four sections. The first, **What is Creativity?**, has two chapters. In Chapter 1, 'The key elements of creativity', the definition of creativity and the three different types of creativity in education are outlined and discussed. The potential benefits and drawbacks of a more creative approach in the classroom are considered for both teachers and their pupils. In Chapter 2, 'Creativity in education: History and theoretical background', the changing place of creativity in the primary school curriculum over the past decades is outlined and the reader is introduced to the work of some of the key researchers and theorists in the area. The place of creativity in primary schools at the present time is examined in this context.

Part Two, **A Creative Child in a Creative Classroom**, unpicks the skills children will need to develop in order to work creatively and the techniques teachers can use to develop those skills. In Chapter 3, 'Building the skills to work creatively', learning and thinking skills crucial to working creatively are considered, including learning stamina, trial and improvement, generating ideas, group-work and communities of enquiry. Chapter 4, 'Establishing the ethos', considers how a creative classroom ethos is established, looks at the influence of classroom layout and organisation, and examines the importance of relationships, motivation and autonomy to learning creatively and learning to be creative. Supporting and scaffolding creative learning are also considered.

The skills and attributes a teacher will need, both to teach creatively and encourage the development of creativity in their pupils, are the subject of Part Three, **A Creative Teacher**. In Chapter 5, 'What makes a creative teacher?', the key knowledge, skills and interactions that a teacher needs to teach effectively, both creatively and to foster creativity, are examined. These include the teacher modelling creative working processes personally and being able to identify, foster and encourage creativity in others. Chapter 6, 'Key skills for the creative teacher', looks in more depth at particular skills that are useful to the creative teacher, including facilitating, questioning, using a sketchbook/ scrapbook approach, motivating and using drama techniques. It also includes issues such as knowing when to follow children's interests and when to 'stick to the plan', the importance of good subject knowledge, and being able to manage time and make time for extended pieces of work.

Part Four, **A Creative Curriculum**, examines in two chapters how to plan for creative outcomes and how to plan in cross-curricular ways, including how to plan with parallel learning objectives, knowing when to make links and when to teach subjects discretely. Chapter 7, 'Planning and assessing for creative outcomes', looks in particular at using key elements of creativity in planning individual lessons. It shows how creative elements can be added to a more standard lesson and highlights additional considerations from research. Chapter 8, 'Medium-term planning for creative outcomes', extends this to medium-term planning. It looks at how a teacher can assess what creative learning is happening and includes a checklist of questions to inform the planning process. The final chapter in this part, 'Case studies: Creativity in practice', examines a range of different case studies analysing the creative techniques used. These include 6 and 7 year olds going on a quest, maths in a shoe shop, and a year-long exploration of culture and identity.

A final section of the book, 'Conclusion and Forward Planning', will briefly round up the main points and offer activities to reflect, set goals, and forward plan to achieve these.

Additional features

Alongside the text there are ideas for the reader to reflect on, examples of classroom practice, and activities for use either individually or in groups. These activities are designed to be used either as self-study or in workshop or INSET sessions and are aimed at Honours (H) level.

At the beginning of each chapter there are links to identify which of the Teachers' Standards are addressed in the chapter: 21 of the 35 standards in the 'Teaching' section are covered by the book and taking part in the activities throughout the book would cover another two. At the end of each chapter there is a summary of the chapter content and a section for further study outlined below. Full lists of references can be found at the end of the book.

Concluding each chapter is a section for further study. This section aims to offer the reader who wants to explore the subject in greater depth the opportunity to do so. It is aimed at Master's (M) level and will provide a progressive and cumulative exercise in critical reflection. The activities will be based on the content of each chapter throughout the book.

Making a start

 Personal thought and reflection

An internet search for quotations on or definitions of creativity will produce scores of results. They can themselves be a stimulus for creative thought, making connections or challenging your preconceptions. Try a search and see what you find. Do the quotes connect with your ideas about education in any way? How do they make you feel? Which excite you and which do you want to argue with?

(Continued)

(Continued)

After reading this book, return to this activity and see if you think differently about the quotes. Do any of them connect with theories you have read about? Do they provide a challenge to you to change your practice or reaffirm changes you are already making?

Here are some to start with:

'I can't understand why people are frightened of new ideas. I'm frightened of the old ones'. **John Cage**

'Education is not the filling of a pail but the lighting of a fire'.

William Butler Yeats

'You cannot use up creativity. The more you use, the more you have'.

Maya Angelou

'Imagination is more important than knowledge'. **Albert Einstein**

'Some look at things that are, and ask why. I dream of things that never were and ask why not?'. **George Bernard Shaw**

PART 1

WHAT IS CREATIVITY?

This section introduces the whole area of creativity to give you a clear understanding of what it is and how it can be applied in primary education. The key elements of creativity are identified and we begin to explore the way they might manifest themselves in a primary classroom. The three different types of creativity in education are outlined and discussed, and the potential benefits and drawbacks of a more creative approach in the classroom are considered for both teachers and their pupils. The changing place of creativity in the primary school curriculum over the past decades is outlined, and you will be introduced to the work of some of the key researchers and theorists in the area. The place of creativity in primary schools at the present time is examined in this context.

CHAPTER 1

THE KEY ELEMENTS OF CREATIVITY

 Learning objectives in this chapter:

- To understand the three different types of creativity in education
- To know how creativity has been defined
- To recognise the key elements of creativity
- To consider the potential benefits and drawbacks of a more creative approach in the classroom

Relevant Teachers' Standards for this chapter

A teacher must:

3   Demonstrate good subject and curriculum knowledge

3b   demonstrate a critical understanding of developments in the subject and curriculum areas, and promote the value of scholarship

Ask a group of teachers what they mean by creativity and you will get a huge range of responses. Creativity means very different things to different people, and in terms of the primary classroom teachers can often find it hard to envisage what it actually looks like, let alone plan to encourage or foster it. This chapter will clarify the concepts so that we can be sure we are understanding creativity in the same way.

 ### Individual or group activity

(Potential activity spoiler! Cover the paragraph beneath this box.)

In just two minutes, think of as many words or phrases as you can that mean 'creativity' to you. Think of creativity in its widest meaning, not just in terms of schools.

   If you were working in groups, share what you came up with. Can you recognise any common themes that have emerged?

When groups of teachers are asked to do the above activity their lists often contain the following: thinking 'outside the box', self-expression, having new ideas, being a risk-taker, imagination, fun, making something new, music, dance, art, drama, inventing, working together, innovation, individuality.

Already, certain strands will be appearing. Firstly, there is the element of newness – of making or thinking something for the first time. Much of the early research into creativity was undertaken by considering genius, and obviously the great names of innovation in art or science demonstrated their creativity by being the first in their field ever to do or discover something. In children it is more likely that their creativity will show the first time *for them* that they have done or discovered something. Having said that, one of the joys of working with primary age children is that sometimes they will say or do something so new and so fresh that they will make you look at the world in quite a different way. Anna Craft (2000) has used the terms 'big c' and 'little c' creativity to differentiate between the types of creativity that change the world's perceptions in significant ways and the types that everyone can practise in their everyday lives.

Another strand is that of creativity in expression or of communicating ideas in creative ways. Perhaps here the ideas are not necessarily new but are being presented in new and original ways. Linked here may well be the idea that creativity gives something of the self, that the ideas are personal and individual. Creativity is not, however, the domain for either strictly individual or exclusively group work. It can cover both of these and we will be looking at this in later chapters.

The elements of individuality and newness also imply a 'difference' to the status quo. People who are creative are, by definition, not conforming to tried and tested ways of doing things. This can be hard for primary age children to deal with and there are issues of conformity and risk-taking that teachers will have to address in their classrooms.

Many people would equate creativity mainly, or even exclusively, with the arts. Although the arts media are highly creative areas there is huge potential for creativity in all the other subject and curriculum areas.

Finally, the word 'fun' often emerges. While, hopefully, much creative work and working creatively will be fun, there will, by its very nature, also be times when this is difficult and frustrating, and for some children more open-ended activities can be extremely stressful. All of the above issues will be dealt with in subsequent chapters in more depth.

Definitions of creativity

After sharing first thoughts about what creativity means to us, let us consider the definitions of creativity that have been most prominent in recent years.

In 1998 the government set up the National Advisory Committee on Creative and Cultural Education (NACCCE). Its report, *All Our Futures: Creativity, Culture and Education* (NACCCE, 1999), proved to be one of the most significant contributions to the debate about creativity, and its importance will be looked at further in the next chapter. This report was specific in its definition of creativity and that definition was subsequently used in a number of government initiatives and other publications:

> Imaginative activity fashioned so as to produce outcomes that are both original and of value. (NACCCE, 1999: 30)

This definition, as can be seen, has four distinct parts:

- Using imagination.
- Pursuing purposes.
- Being original.
- Judging value.

When using the term 'imagination' in relation to creativity the implication is that it is more than fantasising. It incorporates all the aspects of 'newness' in what people see as creativity, including originality. So, it is not only about envisaging completely new ideas but also seeing things in a new light, seeing alternatives to the way things are usually done, or combining things in unusual ways. We often use the term 'creative cook' about people who do not necessarily invent entirely innovative dishes but do not follow a recipe slavishly, who put in a dash of this or a sprinkle of that to give something a new 'twist'. You might also recognise this kind of approach in visual terms, for example there are many people who can put together a 'look' in the way they dress by combining elements you might not usually think would go together, or in home furnishing where selecting and positioning things in particular ways give a sense of style that other people might never be able to achieve. We can look out for this sort of imaginative approach in children in a variety of contexts.

 Individual activity

Think about a group of children you have observed. Have you noticed children who see things in a fresh, new way? Have you been surprised by the method a child has used in a maths investigation, or the way a child has described something that worked well but was out of the ordinary?

Anna Craft calls this kind of imaginative activity 'possibility thinking' (Craft, 2000: 3). It involves the sort of thinking that asks questions such as 'What if ... ?', 'What would happen if ... ?', 'Suppose she ... ?'.

This leads us to the idea of creativity having distinct purposes or outcomes. Creativity doesn't happen in a vacuum, a creative act happens when someone wants to try something or make something happen. It might, of course, turn out that other ideas occur during the process or that the ultimate outcome differs from what was first envisaged, but there is always the intention to do something or make something or try something out. This process can be very playful. Many a great discovery has been the result of playfulness with ideas or materials by the inventor. In the realm of the classroom this has many implications for time management and planning, which we will return to in later chapters.

Creativity happens in a particular medium or combination of media. It therefore demands skills in those media to be creative with. So, a child's great idea about building a model of a tower to fit a particular land site will come to nothing if they don't have the skills to join the component parts together strongly enough. A group wanting to create a piece of music representing the sea will not be able to communicate their ideas if they cannot use their instruments to make the sounds they imagine. Creativity maintains a balance between structure and freedom, between the linear and logical and the random or chaotic.

Being original involves putting oneself on the line, so to act creatively necessitates having a range of personal attributes. A measure of self-confidence is also essential: we must be able to be prepared to have a go at things, and to recognise that our attempts may not work out and to have persistence and the ability to bounce back if things do not go to plan. Although things can be created in solitude at some stage they have to see the light of day and be shared with their audience – this requires risk-taking too and the confidence to accept feedback. Even accepting praise and being the focus of attention can be hard for some people.

The final part of the NACCCE's definition is of judging value. This is a particularly difficult area to judge in a primary classroom. It begs questions such as valuable to whom? What sort of value? Who is to be the judge? The report itself makes the point that just being original is not enough as this may be impractical or not fit for purpose: 'The outcome of imaginative activity can only be called creative if it is of value in relation to the task at hand' (NACCCE, 1999: 33). However, history is full of acts of creativity that were not valued at the time and disregarded. In the classroom what is needed is to foster and develop methods of critical evaluation. Firstly, ideas and outcomes can be evaluated as to whether they met the criteria set at the outset. Depending on the type of creative activity, this may involve whether it is fit for purpose: is it useful or enjoyable, does it communicate particular ideas or feelings? Different points of view can and should be taken into consideration, and even if a particular outcome is deemed not to meet the original intention, the process of evaluation should go on to consider whether it has properties that could be useful in another situation.

You might hear statements such as:

'I didn't see it was a snail, I thought it was a dragon breathing fire.'

'It was meant to be a snail but it came uncurled. I like the idea of it being a dragon; I'm going to paint it with scales and fire.'

'I think we put in too much water so it's not vegetable stew any more, it's vegetable soup.'

Children need to be able to ask these questions of themselves as they are working, they need to become their own 'first marker', to trust their own judgement and to discard, adapt or pursue ideas as they think fit. Self-evaluation should be a constant process throughout a piece of work.

 Classroom idea

Learning skills, design & technology

It is always worth sharing stories with children about pieces of developmental work that appear to fail but turn out to have other uses. One good example here is Post-It notes. The glue on these, which is 'low-tack' and allows repositioning that leaves no mark or residue, was discovered by accident. Its use on small notes was invented by another colleague, who had initially envisaged Post-Its being used as bookmarks.

(Continued)

(Continued)

Other inventions have come from looking at waste. Children in a UK primary school won a competition by inventing an extension tube that could be easily added to the end of pencil stubs to make them reusable.

Encourage children to think about the things they might usually throw away. Is there any way these could be used? What do they look like? What are their properties?

Accustom the children to using 'three stars and a wish' when evaluating any piece of work. They should say three things they like about the piece and have one piece of advice as to how it could be improved. Children should be encouraged to apply this to their own work too. Even if they feel it has failed, what positive elements can they find or what features might be useful when applied to another situation?

Anna Craft (2000) describes the process of creativity as a cycle with five stages. The first is preparation and involves getting into an appropriate physical or mental 'space' where creativity can happen. She then describes a state of 'letting go', of making an empty space where ideas can come, 'surrendering control'. This is followed by germination where the buzz of creation kicks in and ideas abound and there is energy and excitement. The fourth part of the cycle is assimilation. This is an internal stage where ideas take root and gestate, and may happen while doing other things over a period of time. The final stage is completion, where the ideas are honed and brought to fruition (2000: 32, 33).

Individuals may not be aware of all these stages and working in a group may change some of them, but what can be seen is that it is very difficult to expect someone to create something to order at a specific time in a specific place, and yet this is what we tend to do in schools. As teachers we need to see how we can build in time for reflection, for ideas to germinate, and also how we can accommodate an individual who has reached a stage where an idea really needs to be worked on.

Creativity in the classroom

Having looked at the most prevalent definitions of creativity we may be clearer about what is involved, but when people talk about creativity in terms of the primary classroom they can mean several different things.

They may mean **teaching creatively**. This phrase is defined in the NACCCE report as 'using imaginative approaches to make learning more interesting and effective' (NACCCE, 1999: 89). It is often linked with a 'creative curriculum' and used to signify a teacher who may work in the following ways:

- Putting the learning within authentic contexts, using real-life situations wherever possible.
- Making links and connections between different subject areas where these occur naturally.
- Using a variety of teaching methods, including some that might involve working in role or as a facilitator.
- Using time flexibly within the day so that children may be less aware of particular 'lessons'.
- Expecting children to work in a variety of different groupings and with a variety of different outcomes.
- Being flexible in approaches, listening to children's ideas, and being willing to follow them when appropriate.
- Using a variety of approaches to assessment at different levels.

Using some or any of the above doesn't necessarily make you an effective teacher; there are any number of considerations about purpose, context, content, progression and appropriateness to take into account.

 ### Individual or group activity

What is the difference between 'creative teaching' and a 'creative curriculum'? Can you teach creatively within a more formal curriculum? What implications are there for pedagogy if a school wants a 'creative curriculum'? Have you seen examples of schools where this works well or not so well? What were the features?

Hold on to these issues as they will be returned to later.

 ### Individual or group activity

Look at a couple of different medium-term plans. Ask yourself the following questions:

- Is there any way of ascertaining the aims or values of the school from the plan?
- Is there an attempt to make links and connections between subjects? How successful do you think these are?
- Does the plan give any indication of preferred teaching and learning styles? Have you seen any planning at this level which does?

If you wanted to teach creatively using one of these plans, would any be preferable? Why? What are your first ideas about what you might teach and how you might teach it?

There will be much more detail about teaching creatively in subsequent chapters – this is just to start you thinking.

Learning creatively is a relatively new consideration in the literature on creativity in education (see Craft, 2005; Jeffrey and Craft, 2004). It is strongly linked to ideas about pupil autonomy and pupil voice. A child who learns creatively will be involved in understanding how they learn and how they learn best. They will use and develop that knowledge to be involved in devising some of their own learning experiences; they will make suggestions about what the class might do and how they might do it. They will be developing skills in self-evaluation and the evaluation of others' performances.

So, from a creative learner you might hear:

'Can I draw it out first? I think it would be clearer like that.'

'Would an exploded diagram be better? We could write notes on it.'

'If we did a survey we could be sure how many people think that. We can't just assume everyone agrees with us.'

'Will we get a chance to find out about the ships they used? Could I make a model of one? If I made it to scale could I show it in relation to a modern cross-channel ferry?'

'I really like the way he's set it out, it makes it easy to see the connections. I'm going to try it like that.'

The third way creativity may appear in a primary classroom is **teaching to develop creativity**. There is some debate as to whether if you teach creatively you are necessarily also encouraging creativity in the children you teach (Craft, 2005; Jeffrey and Craft, 2004), but it seems most likely that the two will often happen simultaneously. However, when starting out as a teacher or deliberately trying to develop more creativity in your teaching and the children you teach, it would be useful to separate the two in your mind. This is especially important when you are planning so that you can be aware of the elements of creativity you want to foster and develop in the children you teach and plan an appropriate stimulus and activities to achieve this.

This takes us back to the key elements of creativity and our task will now be to find ways that we can foster and develop these elements both within ourselves as teachers and in the children we teach.

The key elements of creativity

Taking ideas from the definitions of creativity and the sharing of teachers' own experiences, we can identify a list of the key elements of creativity:

- Generating new ideas.
- Applying known skills and ideas in different contexts.

- Taking other people's ideas or starting points and moving them on or personalising them.
- Communicating ideas in interesting or varied ways.
- Putting different or disparate ideas together to make something new.
- Working towards a goal or set of goals.
- Evaluating their own or others' work.
- Adapting and improving on their work in the light of their own or others' evaluations.

Let's now put these in the context of a primary school classroom by considering how they may appear in practice.

Generating new ideas

These ideas may be in any subject area and need only be new to the child themself. Think about ways of moving differently in PE; composing a melody; drawing a conclusion from evidence in a science investigation or from historical evidence; making a generalised statement from individual observations, maybe in a maths investigation; designing an implement or a recipe; thinking up a plot for a story and so on. In Chapter 3 we will look at some methods to help children develop their own ideas.

Applying known skills and ideas in different contexts

This may involve using something you have learned and applying it to a completely different subject or situation. For example, children may have real-life experience that cooking a sloppy mixture of flour, egg, sugar and liquid can make crunchy biscuits, but will never before have applied this knowledge to a scientific understanding of reversible and irreversible changes. Observing mini-beasts might lead to their applying the way these move to a dance or the way a moving vehicle is designed, and features of their appearance might be used to design a suit of clothes.

Taking other people's ideas or starting points and moving them on or personalising them

This can often happen naturally when working in a group. You may hear children's ideas tumbling over each other so that it is not clear exactly who had the original idea:

'We could make it like a battle.'

'Yeah, but in slow motion.'

'Nobody actually touches anyone else.'

'With spins and kicks, like kung fu.'

'But really slow.'

In the above conversation about a proposed dance only the final comment is not actually moving on the idea – all the other participants were adding their own creative contribution.

Sometimes longer has to be spent getting to know another person's methods or ideas before they can be personalised. Peter Dixon is rightly scathing about the value of 'rows of six-year-olds copying rather obscure paintings by Kandinsky, for no other reason than they have been told to do so' (quoted in Alexander, 2010: 227). However, there is a place for examining and practising the techniques of 'masters' before using and perhaps adapting these in creating a new work. In Chinese culture there might be years of imitation of a master artist before a student was considered skilled enough to develop their own ideas. We tend, in the West, to value individuality more and earlier, but should not underestimate the creative possibilities of building on ideas and techniques of others, be they acclaimed in their field or by our peers.

Communicating ideas in interesting or varied ways

As teachers we tend to ask children to communicate their ideas and knowledge mostly in words and more often than not in written words. It is not unusual when asking a colleague about a child's ability in science to be told about their difficulties in reading and writing. If that teacher only assesses children's learning through their written work they cannot see past the difficulties in writing to recognise what the child knows and understands about the science concepts. In some cases a child may be very able in science and this may not be being recognised. This is just one of the reasons that communicating in different ways can be valuable.

Try asking children to illustrate either a passage of fiction or non-fiction including as much information as they can from the passage in their picture; this shows you clearly what they have understood. Can they use movement to demonstrate the action of molecules in solids, liquids and gases? Can they make a model of a Roman town or a diagram to show how to make something?

Putting different or disparate ideas together to make something new

This is similar to applying knowledge in different contexts but in this case two or more things are combined to make something new. Some forty years ago there was a new invention called 'splayds', which were essentially forks with a cutting edge on one side enabling you to eat with one implement.

They never caught on, but someone had had the idea of combining the two features. Or what about composing fusion music combining two different genres or designing a dish that incorporates food from two different cultures?

Working towards a goal or set of goals

Of course almost everything that happens in a classroom will have some sort of goal or expected outcome. In this context, though, we are thinking about setting children a challenge that they have to work towards. That challenge will involve a number of different stages and necessitate the children planning various activities to achieve their goal. This will often mean that they identify for themselves what they need to learn as they go along and therefore are highly motivated to achieve that learning. It also often places the learning in authentic 'real-life' contexts. For example, challenges might involve planning a party for their class, producing 200 copies of a school newspaper on a certain day, starting and maintaining a recycling scheme. These challenges will generally involve learning and applying skills in a number of different subject areas and will also require a variety of different learning and social skills.

Evaluating their own or others' work

This was discussed earlier in terms of judging value. It is really important that this becomes an integral part of how children work and think at all stages. If it is only done at the end of a piece of work then it can just feel like an 'add-on' activity and the possibility of changing direction more fruitfully will be lost. From the moment ideas are generated they have to be evaluated to determine which are to be selected and worked on further.

Adapting and improving on their work in light of their own or others' evaluations

This is strongly linked to the point above and shows a commitment to improving their work as they go and in the future. Obviously it is important for teachers to judge at what stage stopping and celebrating their achievements is appropriate for individuals, groups or the whole class. Celebrating success and knowing what that feels like are just as important as recognising how you can improve.

Creativity in the Early Years

One of the best places to see all these key elements of creativity in action is in an Early Years setting. Young children are naturally creative and the strong interrelationship between play and creativity has meant that Early

Years provision has fostered creative learning strongly. As Paulette Luff points out in her chapter 'Play and Creativity', 'Neither 'play' nor 'creativity' can be easily defined but qualities of imagination, exploration, freedom and flexibility are common to both, and this accounts for their significance within Western traditions of early years education' (Luff, in Waller and Davis, 2013: 129).

In recent decades the influence of the Reggio Emilia approach to pre-school experiences has become more evident with many Early Years practitioners adopting the principles. Amongst these principles are those of seeing the child as someone who is already capable and has skills and competence; the cooperation and collaboration between the child, its parents and the teacher; seeing the learning environment as the 'third teacher', a strong participant in the world of learning being created; the pursuit of often long-term projects which are generated by the children's interactions and enquiries; and the careful observation, documentation and analysis of each child's learning in a number of different ways. There are many articles online or published which discuss the Reggio Emilia approach to Early Years learning and these are well worth looking at. You might try *The Hundred Languages of Children: The Reggio Emilia Approach to Early Childhood Education* edited by Edwards et al. (1993, Ablex).

 Individual or group activity

Spend some time observing in an Early Years setting. Which of the key elements of creativity can you see in action? How do the adults interact with the children? It may help you to take a list of the key elements of creativity with you as you observe.

When you reflect on your observations discuss or list which of the key elements of creativity you saw in action. What were the main features of the way learning was happening?

You may well have observed a very playful environment with children having time to experiment with ideas, equipment and materials without a set 'outcome'. Learning will most likely have crossed subject boundaries and children will have been applying knowledge and skills from one area to another. There was probably a carousel of activities so that staff could concentrate on some small groups at times. The setting was more than likely a rich educational resource with indoor and outdoor areas and many interesting things to touch, feel, see and interact with at the children's level.

Take some time to consider which of the elements you observed you could adapt for older children. How would this make their learning more interesting and effective?

As you continue through this book you will find many points which relate back to Early Years practice. Make as many opportunities as you can to continue your visits to the youngest learners – these can often help us clarify what is important about how children learn and the experiences which can best help this.

What are the benefits and potential drawbacks of creativity in the classroom?

It is probably evident by now that there are a lot of different aspects to consider if you want to teach more creatively or help children become more creative. Before we continue to look at those aspects it is worth considering why we value creativity and what we believe it can achieve for young people and for ourselves as teachers. It would also be unwise to ignore the fact that working creatively or to encourage creativity can have drawbacks or involve difficulties that will need to be overcome. Looking at those drawbacks clearly can help you either to deal with them straightaway or to decide to wait until you are more experienced before tackling that particular aspect.

 Individual or group activity

(Potential activity spoiler! Cover the paragraphs beneath this box.)

Draw two columns (one for positives and one for negatives) and list as many positives and negatives as you can for both teaching creatively and teaching to develop creativity.

 Group activity

Choose one positive and one negative and prepare to communicate these to the other groups. You should try to communicate in ways other than explaining in words. You could do a role play to share your idea or use modelling material to make a symbolic representation, you could draw a poster or a picture, create a short dance or a poem. After a short preparation time, share your different positives and negatives. The group sharing should try not to explain what they have done until the audience has had time to discuss what it could mean. Often, the audience will come up with points that were not intended by the performers but are valid and useful.

Discuss and 'unpick' the points raised plus any from your original lists that were not illustrated in the sharing activity.

Below are some of the points that often come up when students and teachers undertake this activity. Note that these lists are not exhaustive.

Positives/Benefits

- Children tend to remember things better if they learn them in creative, interactive ways.
- It caters to different learning styles, children can access learning in a variety of ways.

- It allows children to demonstrate their learning in ways that are not just through reading and writing.
- It raises the self-esteem of children, particularly those for whom reading and writing are difficult.
- It is more fun.
- Children have more autonomy over their learning and get more personal fulfilment.
- It is useful. Creativity is valued in society and it builds skills for future learning.
- It puts learning in authentic or 'real-life' situations. It is meaningful to children.
- It enhances motivation and builds skills in 'learning to learn'.
- It is more fulfilling for teachers.

Negatives/Drawbacks

(with some brief comments – these issues will be dealt with in subsequent chapters)

- **Time management.** This is a very real issue on a number of levels. How do you manage to find the time for extended pieces of work? How do you cope when some children have finished but others are still involved in meaningful exploration? How do you find any time within the constraints of the curriculum?
- **Unconventionality.** Being creative involves encouraging thinking that is not just following the crowd and behaviours such as relishing doing things in different ways. How does this fit with the peer pressure to conform? Or knowing when you have to do things exactly the same as other people and when you are expected to be individual?
- **Mess.** Lots of teachers worry that working creatively is inherently messy! Hopefully from your reading thus far you will realise that creativity is more about ways of thinking and enquiry than glue and sequins. However, if mess is involved, you can train children to care for resources and be good at tidying up.
- **Parents and/or senior managers not understanding; a lack of written work in books.** Hopefully you will be working within a school that values children learning in this way and has an outward-looking policy to help parents understand how their child is learning. There are lots of ways, however, of recording and assessing creative work in different media, of focusing on metacognition so that the children recognise what and how they are learning and don't go home saying 'We just played today.'
- **Making sure you have 'covered it all'.** Teaching creatively is not an easy option and a creative teacher needs to know the curriculum well, be able to make decisions about when and how it is the right time to explore something, and be responsible for making sure there is a balance between structure and flexibility.

- **The 'blank sheet' moment.** Being asked to come up with your own individual ideas, often at a moment's notice, can be very threatening. Learning creatively needs to be structured and scaffolded in exactly the same way as any other method of learning. There are skills involved in being creative that have to be learned and teachers need to build these skills and children's confidence gradually.

Final thoughts

Being creative in one way or another is a human characteristic. We all have the potential to be creative: we make things, we solve problems, we want to understand how things work or make them work better. We may have natural propensities to learn better in certain areas but we can all learn to improve our skills across the board. Teachers are creative, it is part of the job, but outstanding teachers are highly creative.

Chapter summary

In this chapter we have examined our own ideas about what creativity is and some definitions of creativity in education, particularly the very influential definition in the NACCCE's (1999) report. We have identified that there are three types of creativity at work in a primary classroom, namely teaching creatively, learning creatively, and teaching to develop creativity. The key elements of creativity were identified and introduced and possible benefits and drawbacks to teaching more creatively or encouraging more creativity in the classroom were identified prior to looking at these in more detail in subsequent chapters.

 Personal thought and reflection

- In what ways are you personally most creative?
- Who is the most creative teacher you have observed so far? What were the features of their practice?
- Did you or your group come up with more positives or negatives in your listing activity?
- Do you personally feel there was more 'weight' to one side or the other? Can you identify why that is?

Further study

This section aims to offer readers who want to explore the subject in greater depth the opportunity to do so. Completing the activities in this section for each chapter will provide a progressive and cumulative exercise in critical reflection. Each activity is based on the content of the chapter.

About critical reflection

Critical reflection involves a number of different strands which will be introduced in the activities following each chapter. This might involve writing a synthesis of a paper – namely summarising, pulling out or drawing together the main message. It might involve evaluating either a research paper, your own teaching, or a child's learning. The evaluation could involve assessing strengths and weaknesses, how valid the judgement is or how reliable the evidence is. It might also involve analysis: for example, parts of a problem might be broken up to look at solutions. You might test out ideas or interpretations and extrapolate various ways of looking at a situation, challenge the assumptions or hypotheses suggested, or speculate on a solution.

Reflection is a vital skill for teachers, enabling theoretical ideas to be brought together with all that is seen, heard or experienced in practice. For example, seeing someone actually helping a child to learn something new by using a supportive technique may lead to understanding 'scaffolding' learning from a different perspective from that of the understanding gained when reading Vygotskian theory or Bruner's work on the subject.

Critical reflection: Activity 1

Allow an hour for this activity.

In one short paragraph *identify* the three different types of creativity discussed in this chapter.

Identify one occasion when you have been in a position of learning creatively. In a few sentences *describe* objectively the context of this experience. *Explain why* you consider this to be a situation where you were learning creatively.

Take time to remember this experience. Where were you? Who was with you? What were you doing? What were you feeling as you were learning?

Now write a brief evaluation of this experience. One way of doing this is to *identify* what helped you. What was useful? What was positive?

Now *identify* and *examine what* changed in you as a result of this experience or *what* you see differently and *how* it will make you change some aspect of your classroom practice. It may be appropriate here to take time with some aspect of the experience that was challenging or that you found unhelpful and write a paragraph about *what* was challenging, *why* it was challenging, and *what* you learnt from that.

Remember:

- Reflection should take you forward. Ruminating or dreaming goes round in circles whereas reflection moves you on – you 'see' something in a new light.
- Writing after a time of reflection can help you crystallise your learning and move your thinking on to a new stage.
- Reflective writing is not very descriptive – you provide just enough description to set the context for your analysis.

Further reading

Craft, A. (2000) *Creativity across the Primary Curriculum*. London: Routledge.

Edwards, C. et al. (eds) (1993) *The Hundred Languages of Children: The Reggio Emilia Approach to Early Childhood Education*. New York: Ablex.

Jeffrey, B. and Craft, A. (2004) 'Teaching creatively and teaching for creativity: distinctions and relationships', *Educational Studies*, 30 (1): 77–8.

NACCCE (National Advisory Committee on Creative and Cultural Education) (1999) *All Our Futures: Creativity, Culture and Education*. London: DfEE.

CHAPTER 2

CREATIVITY IN EDUCATION:
HISTORY AND THEORETICAL BACKGROUND

 Learning objectives in this chapter:

- To understand the changing place of creativity in the primary school curriculum over the past decades
- To be introduced to the work of some of the key researchers and theorists in the area
- To consider the place of creativity in primary schools at the present time

---

Relevant Teachers' Standards for this chapter

A teacher must:

3   Demonstrate good subject and curriculum knowledge

3b   demonstrate a critical understanding of developments in the subject and curriculum areas, and promote the value of scholarship

---

In the past few decades creativity has been both out of and in fashion in educational theory, policy and practice. In this chapter we look at the place creativity has occupied both today and in past decades in the primary school curriculum.

The background

Anna Craft is one of the educationalists who has written most about creativity in recent years. She identifies a first and second 'wave' of creativity in education (Craft, 2005). The first wave she characterises as the period during the 1960s when the Plowden Report was published and there was considerable attention focused on child-centred education. The 1967 report of the Central Advisory Council for Education, chaired by Lady Plowden, was published as *Children and their Primary Schools*. It is best known for stressing that 'at the heart of the educational process lies the child' (Central Advisory Council for Education, 1967: 7). The report was based on the Piagetian theory of developmental sequence and proposed methods of education in line with children's physical and intellectual development. These methods introduced more play-based learning for younger children, and the grouping of subjects into 'topics'.

The second wave came during the late 1990s. It was then that the educational community really started taking notice of creativity – psychologists and educationalists were doing research, reports were commissioned, teachers and school leaders were voicing their interest and government education policy started to reflect this. (These key developments will be outlined in more detail later in the chapter.)

In 1976 the then prime minister James Callaghan gave a speech at Ruskin College, Oxford, which came to be known as the Great Debate. He proposed a national debate about the aims and nature of education, and while he was himself strongly supportive of teachers and schools he outlined several concerns including 'the methods and aims of informal instruction' as against 'the strong case for the so-called "core curriculum" of basic knowledge'. He was also particularly worried about the lack of good science teaching and how promising students were not entering industry as a career. Whether the debate happened in the way Callaghan intended is itself debatable, but it did bring educational issues into the glare of public and government scrutiny which led to a formerly fairly unregulated system becoming far more formally regulated.

In 1989 the National Curriculum was introduced and for the first time children all over the country studied the same curriculum. The 'back to basics' movement which was heralded in the Great Debate gained momentum, with the designation of maths, English and science as 'core' subjects in the National Curriculum and other subjects being known as 'foundation' subjects. Anna Craft, then a project officer at the National Curriculum Council, remembers that 'During the mid- to late 1980s … creativity (along with many other worthy educational objectives, including educational research) was knocked off the agenda as "oldspeak"' (Craft, 2005: 11).

In 1998 and 1999 respectively the Literacy (NLS) and Numeracy (NNS) strategies followed. These became popularly known as the Literacy Hour and Numeracy Hour, and were introduced to schools with a structure of how a lesson should be presented. This was based on recent research and literature on school effectiveness and school improvement (see for example Reynolds, 1998; Reynolds and Muijs, 1999). It emphasised 'interactive whole class teaching' and training provided teachers with step-by-step instruction in this teaching method. This structure became so embedded that it became rather formulaic and was repeated again and again in almost every subject. The four-part format of starter activity, teacher exposition, independent work and plenary, while working perfectly well, meant that lessons could easily become overly predictable.

In 2000 the QCA schemes of work were introduced. Teachers had felt that they and every school in England and Wales were having to create their own schemes of work from the National Curriculum content and had asked for exemplification materials. The QCA schemes of work for the foundation subjects were never statutory but many teachers believed they were. Educational publishers produced materials to support them, making them hard to resist, and adopting them meant that when teachers moved between schools they could pick up the curriculum relatively seamlessly. However, the schemes did result in many teachers becoming used to just picking up a ready-made plan and 'delivering' it without considering the particular needs or interests of the children in their classes. The increasing ease of being able to download a lesson plan directly from the internet added to this tendency. The belief that what was in the QCA schemes of work *was* the National Curriculum persisted and teachers found it easy to lose sight of what was actually in the National Curriculum and just how much scope it gave for creative and flexible approaches.

 Classroom example

History

A teacher with a class of 6 and 7 year olds was finding it hard to teach about Florence Nightingale. Many of the children in her class were new arrivals to the UK, and understanding about someone who had lived so long ago in such a different culture was very difficult for them. The teacher herself did not enjoy the topic but believed she had to teach it.

Once she understood that the curriculum only specified that the children should learn about 'the lives of significant individuals in the past who have contributed to national and international achievements', she felt inspired to choose someone to whom the children in her class would be able to relate more easily.

She started with Dame Anita Roddick (1942–2007), the founder of The Body Shop, as an example of a pioneer of sustainability, environmentalism and human rights in business enterprise. This also fitted well with work on the rainforest which she had planned. She would then choose another significant person from further back in history at a later point in the year when the children's skills and understanding were more developed.

Following the Dearing Review in the 1990s, the primary National Curriculum was slimmed down considerably, but after publication of the revised National Curriculum (DfEE/QCA, 1999) (now known as Curriculum 2000) teachers still felt the curriculum was extremely overcrowded. Most schools had arranged to teach Literacy and Numeracy in the mornings and so the whole of the rest of the curriculum was squeezed into the afternoons. One way of organising it and making sure that every subject got its slot in the timetable was to teach in a very subject-specific way, and this became the norm in a majority of primary schools. By the end of the decade there were a significant number of teachers, parents and children who felt that the creativity, spark and fun had gone out of primary classrooms (see PWC, 2001; Smithers and Robinson, 2001). Teachers have reported that children were behaving differently in different parts of the day. Some felt that the Literacy and Numeracy hours were 'proper learning' and took them seriously, but gave less status to other subjects and so played around in those lessons. Conversely, other teachers reported that children were becoming bored with the rather formulaic Literacy and Numeracy hours, and were much more motivated by the perceived freedom of working on the foundation subjects in the afternoons.

None of this was, of course, a necessary outcome. Many schools and teachers managed to incorporate the new strategies within a vibrant and exciting curriculum and pedagogy. They created learning opportunities for children which challenged and motivated them and were relevant to their lives. However, this was in itself a challenge and involved hard work and dedication at a time when issues of excessive workloads for teachers were high on the agenda. The course of least resistance was to use pre-prepared schemes of work, either those provided by the QCA, NLS or NNS, or those produced by educational publishers.

During the same period of the 1990s there was growing interest in learning and thinking skills. The results of the research in these areas changed many educators' perceptions about how children learn and therefore which teaching and learning styles were appropriate. During this period Howard Gardner published his work on multiple intelligences, arguing that intelligence was not a single capacity but that people had a range of different intelligences, some of which were predominant in each individual (Gardner, 1993). Daniel Goleman showed how the ability to think and learn was inextricably linked to our emotions and could be inhibited by stress, anger or other strong emotions, and that people needed good emotional intelligence to understand themselves and others and develop as rounded individuals who could cope in a variety of situations (Goleman, 1996). Mihaly Csikszentmihalyi identified a state of mind which he called 'flow', where individuals were in a state of deep concentration and learning and creative thinking were most productive (Csikszentmihalyi, 1990). Edward de Bono's thinking strategy of 'thinking hats' of different colours was used in many schools for children to practise and extend their capabilities in thinking in different ways (de Bono, 1999).

All of this was happening at the same time as advances in technology were precipitating huge changes in the world of work and our expectations of employment in the future. In 1998 the government set up the National Advisory Committee on Creative and Cultural Education (NACCCE). This was timed to coincide with the review of the National Curriculum and was chaired by Ken Robinson, then a professor at the University of Warwick. The first section, called *Facing the Future*, outlined the need for workers with the 'ability to generate new ideas rather than to manufacture commodities' (NACCCE, 1999: 19), and throughout this period there was a growing consensus that the country needed to foster creativity to 'keep pace with rapidly changing market conditions' (1999: 19).

So, in the last few years of the twentieth century and the first few of the twenty-first we had a situation in primary schools where teachers often felt they were 'delivering' a curriculum rather than teaching, where classroom practices had tended to become routine but where advances in educational research and psychology were signalling exciting new approaches to teaching and learning, and where government policy sought to encourage creativity in terms of innovation and new technologies.

Creativity became a word that featured more and more often in research and educational policy at all levels.

Creativity in the primary curriculum and government policy

As has been seen, despite the gains from the introduction of the National Curriculum, the NLS and NNS, there was a perception that much had been lost in terms of creativity, a joined-up approach to the curriculum, and time for what were known as the foundation subjects (those other than maths, English, science and, slightly later, Information and Communications Technology (ICT)). This was recognised in the commissioning of a series of reports by the new Labour government in the late 1990s and the resulting inclusion of recommendations in policy at a range of levels.

One of the most influential reports was from the NACCCE mentioned above. This was entitled *All Our Futures: Creativity, Culture and Education* and was published in 1999. While it recognised the need for developing creativity and innovation in the country's future workforce, it also recognised that young people's 'needs are not only academic. They are social, spiritual and emotional. All young people need an education that helps them to find meaning and to make sense of themselves and their lives' (NACCCE, 1999: 24). It also recognised the 'motif of educational debate over the last ten years has been the need to get back to basics', but that 'the transformational changes we have outlined here are enough to raise questions about what these basics are' (1999: 26).

Personal thought and reflection

- Is it important for an education policy to have aims? Why do you think that?
- What do you believe are the aims of education? How much do you feel it is to make young people fit for future employment? What other aims should education have?

 Individual activity

What were the aims of:

- Curriculum 2000?
- the proposed new curriculum resulting from the *Independent Review of the Primary Curriculum* (the Rose Review, 2009)?
- the curriculum proposed by the *Cambridge Primary Review* (Alexander, 2010)?
- the *National Curriculum in England Framework Document* (DfE, 2014)?

How do these differ? What are their similarities? Do they seem to imply anything about their attitude to creativity in its broadest terms?

The NACCCE report outlined a definition of creativity which is discussed in greater detail in the next chapter and it produced 59 recommendations for the government. These make extremely interesting reading as regards the vision of education they portray. In retrospect we can identify the areas that were acted upon and those that did not see the light of day. The main tenor of the recommendations is a call 'to ensure that the importance of creative and cultural education is explicitly recognised and provided for in schools' policies for the whole curriculum and in government policy for the National Curriculum' (NACCCE, 1999: 192). Among the detailed recommendations are calls for 'achieving parity between the following discipline areas throughout key stages 1–4 as a matter of entitlement':

- Language and literacy.
- Mathematics and numeracy.
- Science education.
- Arts education.
- Humanities education.
- Physical education.
- Technological education.

In order to achieve parity, 'the existing distinction between core and founda-tion subjects should be removed' (1999: 196). This is obviously one recommendation that was not acted on and the balance of the curriculum has remained weighted firmly towards literacy and numeracy. There were also recommendations for initial teacher training, calling for 'parity between the arts, sciences and humanities in the training of primary school teachers' and to 'establish a new category of Accredited Teaching Assistant to supple-ment expertise in schools in the field of creative and cultural education' (1999: 197).

Other calls were for funding for more continued professional develop-ment in creative teaching and learning, creative thinking skills, the arts and humanities and teaching for cultural understanding, and that these should be 'priorities for support' (1999: 199). Alongside recommendations for the curriculum were some about the use of formative assessment, and the final two sections were on developing partnerships and encouraging the use of new technologies. These recommendations were taken on board, and as will be seen assessment for learning and the use of new technologies featured strongly in subsequent initiatives. It is, however, in the field of developing partnerships between schools and arts organisations that the NACCCE report is now largely remembered. The Creative Partnerships programme, estab-lished in 2002, was the result of this initiative, and provided support and funding for thousands of projects across the country. However successful they were, the creative partnerships served to perpetuate the idea that crea-tivity was essentially situated in the domain of the arts – a perception that still pertains in many people's eyes.

⟳ Personal thought and reflection

- From your observations in school thus far what is the balance between differ-ent subjects in the curriculum?
- Does this vary much between different schools you have visited or would you consider the balance to be similar in most schools?
- How far does your initial teacher training course model the balance between subjects found in primary schools?
- If the recommendations of the NACCCE report on core and foundation sub-jects had been implemented what differences might be seen in primary schools today? What do you think the results of that might have been?

Another report relevant to creativity in schools was also published in 1999. The then DfEE commissioned a review into the position of 'thinking skills' in the classroom. As a result of the review by Carol McGuinness (*From Thinking Skills to Thinking Classrooms*, 1999) thinking skills became recognised within the revised Key Stage 1 and Key Stage 2 National Curriculum (DfEE/QCA, 1999), with 'creative thinking' as one of the constituent parts.

Within the revised curriculum creative thinking was seen as a 'universal' cross-curricular skill which was 'embedded in the subjects of the National Curriculum' and 'essential to effective learning' (DfEE/QCA, 1999: 20). This built on the Early Years and Foundation Stage curriculum where one of the six areas of learning was creative development, including art, craft and design and imaginative play. The National Curriculum, however, emphasised its cross-curricular applications in all subject areas, thereby ensuring that creative thinking was not held to be the preserve of the arts alone.

Curriculum 2000 became statutory in schools in September 2000. After a couple of years while it settled in and became embedded and the NLS and NNS were similarly becoming established, new moves were made to ensure that the curriculum did not narrow down too much. The three strands were drawn together into what became known as the Primary National Strategy which was launched with the document *Excellence and Enjoyment* (DfES, 2003). This set out the new government's vision for primary education in a way that should have given huge scope for creativity within it.

The strategy document was introduced by the then Minister for Education, Charles Clarke, with phrases such as 'children learn better when they are excited and engaged' and 'when there is joy in what they are doing, they learn to love learning' (DfES, 2003: 2). The executive summary continues in the same vein. The very first paragraph pronounces that 'primary education is about children experiencing the joy of discovery, solving problems, being creative in writing, art, music, developing their self-confidence as learners and maturing socially and emotionally' (2003: 3). It is noticeable here that creativity is placed very much in the realm of the arts, but it was radical in that discovery, creativity and problem solving were seen as the cornerstones of primary education, and that being a good learner and social and emotional skills should be part of that definition of primary school education.

There are also calls in these opening paragraphs for teachers to 'take ownership of the curriculum ... Teachers have much more freedom than they often realise to design the timetable and decide what and how they teach' (2003: 3).

But set alongside these exhortations to 'be creative and innovative' are equally strong ones to 'focus on raising standards' and 'use tests, targets and tables to help every child develop to his or her potential' (2003: 3).

The juxtaposition of these aims in the first six paragraphs of the strategy neatly demonstrates the various pulls and pressures there have been in primary schools from the late 1980s to the present day. One might say from that time educational policy became such a prominent part of political policy in the United Kingdom. There is no doubt that while some schools managed to fulfil this balance of engaging, creative learning within a rich and exciting curriculum with rigorous target-setting and preparing the children for the

National Tests (SATs), there were very many who found themselves under intense pressure to raise test scores in maths, English and science and felt that the only way to do so was to 'teach to the tests'.

Excellence and Enjoyment attempted to demonstrate how successful schools managed to balance all the elements. It is full of examples of good practice and the initial strategy document was followed in 2004 by a comprehensive pack of training materials for schools: *Excellence and Enjoyment: Learning and Teaching in the Primary Years* (DfES, 2004). These materials were divided into three areas (with each then subdivided) which show how the research and reports commissioned in recent years had been used to impact on the advice on teaching and learning in schools.

The three areas highlighted for development were:

- creating a learning culture:

  o conditions for learning
  o classroom community, collaborative and personalised learning;

- planning and assessment for learning:

  o assessment for learning
  o designing opportunities for learning;

- understanding how learning develops:

  o learning to learn: key aspects of learning across the primary curriculum
  o learning to learn: progression in key aspects of learning.

Here was a really positive blueprint for developing learning in creative ways. The learning and thinking skills and social and emotional skills were seen for the first time at the heart of the curriculum as 'key aspects of learning':

- Enquiry.
- Problem solving.
- Creative thinking.
- Information processing.
- Reasoning.
- Evaluation.
- Self-awareness.
- Managing feelings.
- Motivation.
- Empathy.
- Social skills.

As will be seen in subsequent chapters, these key aspects of learning are prerequisites for developing creativity.

However, the timing of *Excellence and Enjoyment*, after all the initiatives of recent years, meant that the materials and documentation remained on many a school shelf unopened. Schools felt they had been 'told how to do it' one time too many and were tired of new government education initiatives. There was also cynicism about how much the hierarchy (often perceived as the government, the local authority and even the head teacher) actually wanted the 'enjoyment' part of the strategy when there were so many mixed messages and so much emphasis on achieving targets in test results and focusing on the 'core' subjects of English, maths and science.

 Group activity

Split into two groups. One group should think of as many reasons as possible why a creative approach and a broad, rich curriculum would be appropriate for a primary class. The other group should take an opposing view and think of as many drawbacks as possible to a creative approach and reasons why, for example, 'teaching to the test' or using ready-prepared lesson plans would be the right approach.

The two groups should then form up into two parallel lines to make a 'conscience alley'. One person should walk slowly between the two lines as everyone else repeats one or two of their reasons to the walker, trying to persuade them of their point of view. Repeat the activity with several people having a turn to be a walker.

Discuss how influential the reasons felt to the walkers. Which would they have been most influenced by and why? Did one side overwhelmingly 'win' for them or did they feel torn by different considerations?

Curriculum development

In 2005, to further support schools and teachers who were trying to develop more creativity in their pupils, the QCA launched a website (now withdrawn) and pack of accompanying resources called *Creativity: Find it, Promote it* (QCA, 2005). The website provided a forum for teachers to share creative lesson plans and ideas. The resources comprised a series of case study video clips of lessons in a variety of schools and a booklet to guide reflection and discussion of the approaches and issues portrayed.

By the time *Creativity: Find it, Promote it* came out many schools were beginning to try to develop a more 'creative curriculum'. This was often seen in terms of wanting a more integrated approach to the curriculum rather than the subject-specific approach that many had adopted. Many schools developed more thematic planning, making links and connections between subjects, and tried to give more emphasis to the foundation subjects. Creativity was something that most teachers said they wanted to see more of. However, as was seen in Chapter 1, there were many conflicting ideas about what creativity was and often a lack of definition as to whether schools were trying to develop a new curriculum, creative teaching, or more creativity in their pupils, and what the difference was.

In Bexley in 2005 a group of head teachers from eight primary schools applied to the DfES's Innovation Unit for funding to develop what they called the Creative Learning Journey (www.creativelearningjourney.org.uk). This was a method for planning the primary curriculum based on the six areas of learning from the Early Years and Foundation Stage curriculum. It was developed by teachers in the Bexley schools and then launched nationally, and continues to be purchased by many schools wanting to introduce a more 'creative curriculum'.

In 2003 the International Primary Curriculum was introduced in the UK. This was organised in a thematic cross-curricular way, and as with the Creative Learning Journey many primary schools bought the planning and methodology as a package to use in their schools. One of the potential pitfalls with adopting a curriculum 'package' like this is that schools can be tempted to adopt the pre-prepared curriculum schemes of work as they stand, without going through the planning process themselves and without considering how they fit with the school's own aims and values, how styles of teaching and learning might need to be addressed, or what the particular needs or interests of their children are. Some schools found they had just swapped one scheme of work for another, probably with more links and connections between subjects but without actually addressing the nature of learning more creatively or learning to be more creative.

The first decade of the twenty-first century generally saw many primary schools wanting to develop more creativity in their pupils and a more holistic curriculum. The understanding of developing personal, learning, thinking and social skills as being crucial to education, as highlighted in the Primary National Strategy in 2003 and placed within the key aspects of learning, became accepted within most primary schools, but the extent to which schools felt they could develop these skills varied enormously, and there were still very mixed messages for schools in the importance being given to raising standards in maths and English test results and how that should be achieved.

Reviews of the primary curriculum

The end of the decade saw the publication of two reviews of the primary curriculum. *The Independent Review of the Primary Curriculum* (often called the Rose Review) was commissioned by the DCSF in 2008 with Sir Jim Rose as its chairman. There was some controversy over this review from the start, not least because it was called 'independent' but was commissioned by the government and given a clear steer as to the areas it was, and was not, to report on. Testing, for example, was outside its remit.

The final report (Rose, 2009) suggested a model of curriculum reform that was very similar to what many schools were already doing, and showed a clear progression to the secondary curriculum which had itself been recently updated. For example, the aims were the same for both primary and secondary schools, namely for children to become:

- successful learners;
- responsible citizens;
- confident individuals.

The curriculum was presented as a set of concentric circles with these aims at the centre. In the next circle were 'essentials for learning and life'. These comprised literacy, numeracy, ICT, learning and thinking skills, personal and emotional skills, and social skills. The focus statement of the learning and thinking skills was:

> Children have the skills to learn effectively. They can plan, research and critically evaluate, using reasoned arguments to support conclusions. They think creatively, making original connections and generating ideas. They consider alternative solutions to problems. (Rose, 2009: 76)

Much of this focus statement is central to being creative.

The *Cambridge Primary Review* was a much wider ranging and independent enquiry into primary education in the UK. The review was initiated and directed by Professor Robin Alexander and the final report, published as *Children, Their World, Their Education* (Alexander, 2010), is a book of over 500 pages, complex and far-reaching in its aims, purpose and recommendations.

Alexander commented that in submissions to the review 'the words "creative" and "creativity" appeared ... more frequently than almost any others' (2010: 226). It was noted that the words 'invariably were regarded positively' but 'were also used somewhat loosely' (2010: 226). Again, we can notice the positive light in which creativity is seen and the lack of clarity in its definition in the many submissions to this large-scale review, in the same way that they are found among individuals in any school staffroom.

When it comes to suggestions for a new curriculum the review marries eight domains of knowledge, skill, enquiry and disposition with fourteen 'educational imperatives' (2010: 267). One of these domains is arts and creativity. As the title would suggest, this links creativity very closely to the arts and uses the definition of creativity created by the NACCCE's (1999) report and discussed in Chapter 1. Despite the placing of creativity with the arts there is also a recognition that the arts is not the sole domain where creativity will lie, and the NACCCE report is again quoted as to creativity being 'equally fundamental to advances in the sciences, in mathematics, technology, politics, business and all areas of everyday life' (cited in Alexander, 2010: 267). In the section introducing the domain of the arts and creativity, the final sentence states, 'we have also stressed that both creativity and imaginative activity can and must inform teaching and learning across the wider curriculum' (2010: 267).

When a new government was elected in May 2010 the new primary curriculum based on the Rose Review and newly delivered to schools was cancelled, and a White Paper on education, *The Importance of Teaching* (DfE, 2010), set out the intentions of education policy and announced a new review of the National Curriculum in England. The White Paper and remit for the curriculum review (DfE, 2011) made little reference to creativity compared to the emphasis on acquiring core knowledge. There were, however, many references to the need for teachers to use their expertise to decide how to teach in order to motivate and inspire children. The previous National Curriculum was said to be 'squeezing out room for innovation, creativity, deep learning and intellectual exploration' (DfE, 2010: 40), and the new curriculum would create 'scope for teachers to inspire' (2010: 40) and 'allow teachers the freedom to use their professionalism and expertise in order to help all children realise their potential' (DfE, 2011: 1). It is stated clearly that 'teachers, not bureaucrats or Ministers, know best how to teach – how to convey knowledge effectively and how to unlock understanding. In order to bring the curriculum to life, teachers need the space to create lessons which engage their pupils, and children need the time to develop their ability to retain and apply knowledge' (DfE, 2010: 41, 42).

The new National Curriculum underwent many changes and revisions in its draft stages and was finally introduced in schools in September 2014. As promised it was slimmed down in many areas and the point was made that the National Curriculum formed only one part of a school's curriculum and that schools were 'also free to include other subjects or topics of their choice in planning or designing their own programme of education' (DfE, 2014: 5). Personal, social, health and economic education (PSHE) were not made statutory but schools were told they should make provision for this and there was no overall mention of thinking or learning skills. In the aims the only mention of creativity was 'to engender appreciation of human creativity and achievement' (DfE, 2014: 6).

At first glance it would seem that the new curriculum was not encouraging creativity explicitly. However, in the 'purpose of study' sections for many of the individual subjects there is more emphasis on creativity and the types of thinking and questioning that it requires. For example, five of the eleven subjects of the National Curriculum mention creativity specifically (mathematics, art and design, computing, design and technology and music). Others mention what we have identified as key elements of creativity such as 'Teaching should equip pupils to ask perceptive questions, think critically, weigh evidence, sift arguments, and develop perspective and judgement' (history) and 'These types of scientific enquiry should include: observing over time; pattern seeking; identifying, classifying and grouping' (science) (DfE, 2014).

So, there is scope and encouragement for teachers to draw out the creative aspects of each subject, to look beyond the content of the National Curriculum and to add to and enhance what is there, to use their skill as teachers to place learning within exciting and creative contexts, and to teach and encourage children to engage with their learning in creative ways. How much teachers will grasp these opportunities remains to be seen.

 Individual activity

Look at the statements written below by teachers in the first months of adopting the new National Curriculum. In your experience of schools you have visited how far do the statements reflect the reality in schools now?

- The new National Curriculum is less prescriptive in its approach and allows a lot more cross-curricular learning.
- It has allowed us to review and reflect upon practices. As a school we have focused on creativity when planning new topics/themes.
- With less detail it allows people to apply more creativity.
- There's a greater emphasis on spelling, punctuation and grammar in English which gives less opportunity for creative writing, drama etc.
- Objectives are broader, allowing teachers to be more creative with their planning.

If you are interested in the history of education and educational policy, Derek Gillard's website entitled *The History of Education in England* (Gillard, 2011) is well worth visiting (www.educationengland/org.uk).

Chapter summary

It can be seen that creativity is something that teachers have valued in their classrooms over the last decades, and to some extent feel has been squeezed out of the curriculum. Successive governments have viewed creativity as something desirable to foster in young people, but the messages as to how this can be achieved have often been mixed. Creativity is still most often seen as being allied to the arts, but there is also a belief that creativity is a 'thinking skill' and that it has its place right across the wider curriculum.

So, understanding just what creativity is and how it can best be incorporated in the primary curriculum and developed in our classrooms is not clear cut. But it is possible.

 Further study

Critical reflection: Activity 2

Allow an hour for this activity.

Access a paper written by one of the theorists referenced in this chapter. Read it several times to get a sense of the key messages. *Identify* the key points of the paper. Write this as a *synthesis*.

Consider your experience of teaching and learning in primary classrooms. Write key points about your experience alongside your synthesis from above.

Take time to *reflect* on these two columns and observe what you notice. Ask yourself some questions about your observation: for example, the text advises ... how do I experience that, how do my class experience this in my teaching?

When you are ready, *analyse* the points that stand out for you from this reflection.

 Further reading

Alexander, R. (ed.) (2010) *Children, Their World, Their Education: The Report of the Cambridge Primary Review.* London: Routledge.

Csikszentmihalyi, M. (1990) *Flow: The Psychology of Optimal Experience.* New York: HarperPerennial.

Gillard, D. (2011) *The History of Education in England.* Available at www. educationengland. org.uk. This website outlines the history of education in England over 1400 years. It includes links to the text of speeches, papers and legislation and important educational theorists.

Goleman, D. (1996) *Emotional Intelligence.* London: Bloomsbury.

PART 2

A CREATIVE CHILD IN A CREATIVE CLASSROOM

In this second section we concentrate on the way children can be creative in their learning. As a teacher you will have to recognise opportunities and plan activities to develop the skills that children need to be creative. We identify those skills and the techniques teachers can use to develop them with examples from classroom practice to place them in a recognisable context.

Learning and thinking skills crucial to working creatively are considered, including learning stamina, trial and improvement, generating ideas, group-work and communities of enquiry. Creativity can only flourish where there is a classroom ethos that encourages and fosters it, so in this section we look at the influence of classroom layout and organisation and examine the importance of relationships, motivation and autonomy to learning creatively and learning to be creative. We also help you consider how to support and scaffold creative learning in the classroom.

CHAPTER 3

BUILDING THE SKILLS TO WORK CREATIVELY

 Learning objectives in this chapter:

- To understand different learning skills – what they are and why they are important
- To understand thinking skills – what they are and why they are important
- To consider how to teach and foster those skills

Relevant Teachers' Standards for this chapter

A teacher must:

2   Promote good progress and outcomes by pupils

2c   guide pupils to reflect on the progress they have made and their emerging needs

2e   encourage pupils to take a responsible and conscientious attitude to their own work and study

(Continued)

(Continued)

4 **Plan and teach well structured lessons**

4a impart knowledge and develop understanding through effective use of lesson time

5 **Adapt teaching to respond to the strengths and needs of all pupils**

5a know when and how to differentiate appropriately, using approaches which enable pupils to be taught effectively

7 **Manage behaviour effectively to ensure a good and safe learning environment**

7c manage classes effectively, using approaches which are appropriate to pupils' needs in order to involve and motivate them

For a child to be able to work creatively there is a whole array of skills, attributes and dispositions that they will need. Many of these are not school- or learning-specific but will be being learned and fostered in a range of situations at home and in the wider world. Many children will come to school with a well-developed 'toolkit' of learning and thinking skills that they may not be aware of but that they have been practising all their lives. There will be, however, a huge range of messages that different children are influenced by and these may well be contradictory and sometimes counter-productive to good learning. Take, for example, a child who has learned that if they throw a tantrum they are likely to get their own way. This may work for them at home but it is not going to help them be a good learner where dealing with frustrations in a positive and determined way is necessary. Similarly, some parents may be reinforcing a very 'right and wrong answer' approach to learning which may make it difficult for a child to be comfortable in an investigative and open-ended activity. It is therefore important that learning and thinking skills are overtly taught in the classroom, and that children understand why these are important and reflect on how they can be applied in a range of situations.

It may seem obvious that learning to be a good learner is a prerequisite of education but it is comparatively recent that teaching learning skills has been considered important and in many schools it is still considered an additional 'extra', something that is nice to do if there is time but might well drop off the end of the 'to do list' of a busy classroom. However, time spent on developing children's learning to learn skills is always time well spent and a skill to use and value for life. There are many different aspects to being a good learner and these need to be introduced in a structured way and consistently reviewed and put into action.

Learning stamina

Perhaps the most important and possibly the most difficult aspect is an understanding that learning is not always straightforward, that it will of its essence be frustrating sometimes. Children may think that they are the only ones finding the learning hard, that other children are cleverer than them and always find learning easy. It is vital that as a teacher you make sure that children understand this feeling of frustration is universal and normal and has nothing to do with their ability. Remember here that it is when you are finding the going tough that you will be able to learn something completely new.

Dealing with this aspect demands a number of approaches. One is establishing a climate in the classroom that not only understands the importance of learning challenges but also positively relishes them.

 Classroom example

Learning skills

A teacher had just taken over a very difficult Year 6 class where several of the boys in particular were prone to angry outbursts when they got 'stuck'. Chair kicking or even storming out of the classroom was not uncommon. When one boy was heard to growl, 'This is rubbish ...' the teacher stopped the class.

'Well done, John,' he called out. 'Everyone, John has just discovered a wonderful learning opportunity!'

The class looked rather confused; they were more used to being told off in these situations. The teacher went on to 'unpick' what John had found difficult. He asked other children to give their ideas as to ways forward. He asked John which ideas he thought might be worth pursuing and teamed him up with another child to investigate one possible way of working.

Some weeks later there was a palpable change in the atmosphere in the class. It was much more positive and there was a buzz of purposeful murmurings as the children worked. Suddenly from across the room a cry went up, 'Sir! Sir! We've just found a wonderful learning opportunity!'

The class erupted into cheers and whooping akin to a game show, but quickly quieted down when the teacher asked what it was they were having difficulty with and began to lead the class to analyse the problem and find solutions.

The children were beginning to recognise and appreciate 'learning challenges'.

One of the myths of creative processes is that a 'creative spark' comes in an instant and a fully-formed idea leaps into being. In fact, as R. Keith Sawyer points out 'Creativity takes place over time, and most of the creativity occurs while doing the work. The medium is an essential part of the creative process, and creators often get ideas while working with their materials' (Sawyer, 2012: 88). Children will need help to recognise that sticking at an activity and working through it will often produce results, and indeed answers that thinking alone might not produce.

When children are working on open-ended, enquiry-based tasks they need to develop 'learning stamina'. Such tasks often do not have clearly defined solutions. If you are trying to find out if there is a pattern discernible in certain data you may not know how many stages to go through to say for sure whether there is a pattern or not – you may have several routes to pursue or will need to decide if the method you have chosen is the right one and whether to go back to the start and try another approach. This way of working requires both persistence and determination. Guy Claxton calls it 'Resilience', one of his 'Four Rs of Learning Power' (Claxton, 2002).

Steps and targets

To help children develop this 'learning stamina' it is important they recognise that jobs generally have several stages to them. Modelling the thinking involved in even the simplest task will be very helpful here. Try breaking down the task stages out loud for children: 'We need to water the plants because I've noticed the soil is very dry and the leaves are beginning to droop. That means finding the watering can, filling it up from the tap, pouring some water onto the soil in each pot, refilling the watering can if necessary, and putting it away afterwards. Is that right? Did I miss anything?' Such sequences of actions may seem obvious, but that sort of ongoing breaking down into 'bite-sized chunks' is just what children have to do with learning tasks.

Some children may find it helpful to list the potential stages of a task first so they can tick these off as they go. This can make large tasks seem less daunting as there are smaller goals to achieve along the way and a way of plotting progress and looking back at exactly what they have done already. In enquiry-based tasks the progression needed may not be obvious to begin with and the list may have to be added to or adapted. Again, this kind of reflection and evaluation needs to become second nature. All too often in classrooms, evaluation is seen only as an activity that happens at the end – i.e. after you have made your model you evaluate how it went and what you might change next time. This can be very frustrating for children, as when they have finished they want it to be done! Encouraging an ongoing reflective practice will be a lifelong benefit. Again, these skills will need to be modelled, from sharing different children's charts or lists and discussing how they are useful to the thinking-out-loud approach ('Hmm, I really thought that putting a box for your book bags by the door would help to keep them tidy but it's not working. We'll have to try to think of something else'.)

These simple interactions with the children may not seem like teaching but they are introducing or reinforcing ways of approaching problem solving in real-life situations throughout the day.

When evaluation at the end of a piece of work does take place it should be undertaken as a real chance to reflect on the learning and plan next steps and future strategies. Rather than the usual 'what went well, what could I improve?' why not ask some different questions. Try, 'What was most frustrating? Why was this?" or 'What was the most interesting thing you learned a) about yourself b) about the subject whilst doing this work?' Rather than giving the children a questionnaire to fill in why not ask them to interview each other in pairs with a set of question prompts, and then ask them to report back on what they and their partner discovered when doing this particular piece of work. Try and find the time to use the information to discuss future strategies and set simple, realistic targets for future work with the children. When they are used to working in this way they may well be able to set targets both for themselves and each other.

In the 'Going for Goals' theme of the SEAL materials (DfES, 2005) there is a progression of activities to help teach breaking a task down into achievable steps, dealing with boredom or frustration, learning how to motivate yourself and understanding persistence and determination. This also looks at role models and how they have overcome obstacles to achieve their goals. Asking adults in school, including yourself, to share stories of developing 'learning stamina' and encouraging parents to do the same will really help young people understand what is involved in being a creative learner.

Trial and improvement

Another part of the investigative process is understanding trial and improvement as a method. Again, this is best modelled by teachers on a regular basis: 'Well, let's try doing that, shall we? What has happened? Why do you think that happened? What could we try instead? Do you think that would work better? Why?' Modelling the language, mind set and thought processes helps children to replicate the process themselves until it becomes second nature. Try to emphasise that when you are investigating it is very unlikely that your first try will work and that you will learn a lot from the trials that give you unexpected results. Encourage children to take notes of each of the stages because the actions that produce the results you are not looking for this time may be useful another time. (That is why it is better called trial and improvement rather than trial and error.) Make sure you use positive language for these trials – they are 'attempts' not 'mistakes', and responses can be 'Oh look, what has happened?' rather than 'Oh no, it didn't work.' Thomas Edison told a good story about his invention of the electric light bulb (retold in the SEAL Y6 Going for Goals materials; DfES, 2005: 14): 'It took 2000 experiments before he finally got it right. When asked by a young reporter how he felt about failing so many times, Edison replied, "Failing! I did not fail. I invented the electric light bulb. It just happened to be a 2000-step process."'

 Classroom idea

Learning skills, design & technology

The learning journey

To show children, and the whole school community, how important these ways of working are you might make a display that celebrates the whole 'learning journey'. Choose an example of the creative process, perhaps a piece of Design and Technology. Caption the work from one child's perspective. For example:

- This was my first design idea.
- Jamie and Ahmed shared some of their ideas with me and I decided to incorporate some of their ideas with mine.
- When we started making I couldn't make the pod turn the way I wanted it to. I got really stuck.
- Ms J suggested I make the mechanism out of K'Nex to see how it might move. That gave me the idea for using gears.

Displaying the process with as much pride as finished results is an important way to help children recognise the stages involved.

Generating ideas

The above example highlights another key skill a child will need in order to work creatively. It may indeed be the most important skill to the creative individual: the ability to generate ideas. We have already seen how Anna Craft considers 'possibility thinking' to be a cornerstone of creativity (Craft, 2005). All of us have probably, at one time or another, been asked to paint a picture, write a story, plan a menu, or even write a message in a greetings card – and been completely devoid of ideas. If this happens once too often, if we feel pressured or uncomfortable, if we are ridiculed or someone is exasperated with us, then that blank piece of paper can become a real 'mental block'. It is not unusual to come across quite young children who have already become convinced that they 'can't do' something on their own or say they have no ideas.

There are several approaches you can take to encourage children to have confidence in their own ideas. Obviously you want to establish the classroom as a place where ideas are appreciated and accepted at face value by everyone in the room. Some teachers like to label their rooms 'The Ideas

Factory' or 'The Thinking Zone', and children will need to be reminded that everyone's views are to be listened to and valued.

 Classroom idea

Thinking skills

You can play a good circle game that encourages the children to elaborate on ideas. Start with thinking about an object such as a chair. The first person says, 'I'm thinking about a very strange chair. It has twisted legs.' The next person will then add something: 'I'm thinking about a very strange chair. It has twisted legs and a shelf to put your drink on.'

You can play this by drawing and explaining as well as remembering.

For children who really cannot bring themselves to generate ideas you can start by giving them three or four to choose from. Working in a group can also help. Give each member of a group of four children an A3 sheet divided into quarters. They draw or write an initial idea and pass the paper on to the next child who adapts or adds to the initial idea if possible or starts a new one. This process is continued until all four have responded to each of the other ideas. The original member now has their own and three other versions to choose from. This takes the pressure off having to come up with one perfect idea by oneself.

In a similar way, children who set themselves very high standards can keep discarding ideas because they feel they are not good enough. They can be encouraged to list every idea, however inappropriate or unworthy they might consider these to be, and then a group of friends can vote on or rank the ideas. The original child undertakes to develop the idea that is ranked first. Children are often surprised by the value others put on ideas they consider to be useless. Asking the 'panel' to explain why they liked a certain idea can also be useful for everyone concerned.

Bringing a half-formed idea into existence can be greatly helped by 'externalising' it. Drawing diagrams and gesturing can actually help to 'form up' the idea: 'Externalizing early ideas, and then manipulating and working with them, contributes directly to the still-emerging and uncertain creative process' (Sawyer, 2012: 137). Encourage children to sketch ideas and show you with their hands and bodies what they intend.

Group work

Not all creative work is necessarily done in a group; it is perfectly possible to be creative independently and the work on persistence and determination above can really help to encourage independent thought. However, the most creative outcomes often come from group participation, where ideas can be sparked off and developed quickly, building on each other's input.

Group work is not easy to get right, though, and has a very specific skill set that needs to be learned. All too often when teachers say children are working in groups they are either just sitting together but working independently, or one or two individuals are dominating the process to the exclusion of all others, or there are so many arguments nothing productive is being achieved at all. That being said, there has been some significant work done in recent years which has added to our knowledge about how to encourage and teach good group-work skills, and many teachers have invested a lot of time in their classrooms in building the ability to work well in teams. The SPRinG (Social Pedagogic Research into Group work) project reported that 'involvement in the SPRinG project had positive effects on pupils' academic progress and higher conceptual learning', and there were 'increases in on-task interactions, more equal participation in learning, sustained interactions and higher level discussions' (Teaching and Learning Research Programme website, 2005; www.tlrp.org.uk).

One particular method that has proved very useful in helping groups to work well is to give each group member a particular job within the group. This might mean that one member is charged with recording what happens, one is responsible for equipment, another for time keeping etc. Giving the group members badges with their particular role helps to make sure everyone respects that role. Children will need to learn how to fulfil their different roles and until they are well used to the method time will need to be spent discussing what each of the different roles involves in advance and reviewing how well this worked afterwards.

Problems in groups should not be ignored or children just moved to be with others they can get on with. Problem solving is not just a skill for investigative work but for human relations too. Try to establish a procedure for resolving issues between individuals, starting with hearing both sides calmly and with demonstrable impartiality and establishing that it is the children's responsibility to work out a solution that suits both parties (or all parties if there are more than two involved). You can help as a facilitator but giving the responsibility to the children for the outcomes will ultimately give them many more skills in dealing with relationships than relying on an adult to mete out 'justice' or rule in favour of one or other. The aim of the solution should be to find a win–win solution, one that makes both sides feel satisfied that their needs have been met and will provide for the situation not to reoccur. For more information and activities to help build these skills look at the 'Getting On and Falling Out' theme in the SEAL materials (DfES, 2005).

Listening and responding

Another key skill for working well in a group involves listening attentively to other people and taking on board what they have said. Children can be so focused on their own idea and what they want to communicate that they will find it hard to relate to others' ideas. There are a number of ways to encourage improvement in this area. The first, which may seem rather unrelated, is to encourage being good at taking turns. Early Years settings generally spend a lot of time emphasising the importance of good turn-taking, but this needs to be fostered and encouraged for many years for it to become second nature. We probably all know adults who are impatient at waiting their turn. Games like board games, 'big' skipping and relays where waiting for your turn is essential are all good vehicles for learning. Waiting for several weeks for it to be your turn to do a job like taking the register to the office shows that sometimes the wait for your turn might be lengthy but it will come in the end. Be sure to praise good waiting and discuss how it feels to wait for something. This can be linked to building perseverance, as both involve understanding delayed gratification.

When you are asking for contributions to a discussion, if you generally have a 'hands-up' policy, ask the children to put their hands down once you have chosen a child to speak and to focus on what that child says. Hands may only go up again when the speaker has finished and children should then either respond to a point already made or say something that will move the discussion on. Encourage children to reply to each other, not just talk to you as the teacher. Train them to say whom they are responding to and why: 'I'd like to agree with Jade's point about keeping animals in cages, but what about dangerous animals that could jump over walls? If the wall's too high you can't see them.'

Community of enquiry

The above activities that foster good listening in discussions are also part of what have been called 'communities of enquiry'. A community of enquiry often starts with a particular stimulus – a picture, a quotation, a poem used to stimulate interest and curiosity and many avenues to discuss and reflect on.

Children are generally sat in a circle and after initially sharing the stimulus have some individual time to think about this and reflect. Was anything particularly puzzling about it? What was particularly interesting? The children are then asked to talk in pairs and come up with a question or comment to share with the group. These are shared and listed and one area is chosen to be discussed at that time. This discussion may be undertaken as a whole group or broken down into smaller groups who report back.

When this method of enquiry is being established the teacher will have a role in facilitating the discussion and helping by demonstrating good listening and attentiveness, asking for children to clarify or extend points or give the reasons for their ideas. Teachers can also show where links and connections are occurring between different aspects of the topic under discussion and where something new has been generated that might be worth pursuing at another time. Demonstrating mental mapping might be a useful way of recording the ebb and flow of the discussion and the links and connections between different contributions.

Useful tactics for building patience and getting a balance of listening as well as contributing can include giving children a certain number of tokens each for chances to speak. If they use up their chances too early or on a point that someone else has made they may regret it later when they have a really important point to make. Children can also be given one 'interruption card' each which allows for making a burning point that really cannot wait. Making a double circle with half the class sitting in an outer ring and half inside can make it easier for the discussion to flow. The inner ring discusses while the outer ring is charged with observing and later comments on the strengths and weaknesses of the discussion. Their roles are then reversed.

Children who become used to thinking and participating in this way also become used to accepting many different viewpoints about a theme or concept. They become more open-minded and ready to deal with open-endedness and uncertainty. They find that things that are unknown or ambiguous can excite their curiosity and desire to dig deeper rather than be frustrating or daunting. Community of Enquiry is closely allied with Philosophy for Children. To discover more about Philosophy for Children a good starting point is the book *Philosophy in the Classroom* by Matthew Lipman and colleagues (1980, Temple University Press). The SAPERE website (www.sapere.org) is also useful.

Thinking skills

The use of a community of enquiry is often seen as a method for building thinking skills. As was mentioned in Chapter 2, it was in the late 1990s that the then DfEE commissioned a review into the position of 'thinking skills' in the classroom. As a result of the review by Carol McGuinness (*From Thinking Skills to Thinking Classrooms*, 1999) thinking skills became recognised within the revised National Curriculum for Key Stage 1 and Key Stage 2 (DfES/QCA, 1999) as:

- information-processing;
- enquiry;
- reasoning;
- creative thinking;
- evaluation.

and were identified as Key Aspects of Learning in *Excellence and Enjoyment* (DfES, 2003).

As well as the above, many other aspects of thinking have been identified, such as sequencing and sorting, classifying, comparing, relating cause and effect, drawing conclusions, questioning, predicting, contradicting, doubting, generating new ideas, problem solving, testing solutions, making decisions, remembering, forming concepts, planning, imagining, and translating thoughts into words (Fisher, 2006; McGuinness, 1999). Like any other skills, these need to be taught explicitly and fostered within a classroom that values such approaches.

Many different strategies have been developed to enhance thinking skills. One of the most often used is de Bono's 'Thinking hats'. In a group enquiry each group member is responsible for a certain type of thinking rather than ranging from one type to another. Each of these types of thinking is represented by a hat of a different colour:

> White hat = information *What do we know?*
> Red hat = feelings *What do we feel?*
> Purple hat = problems *What are the drawbacks?*
> Yellow hat = positives *What are the benefits?*
> Green hat = creativity *What ideas have we got?*
> Blue hat = control *What are our aims?*

To use this approach in the classroom the children will need to have had the approach modelled and to have discussed how each group member is required to think within their own sphere for the duration of the discussion and not to take on someone else's way of thinking. Once they are used to the method they should be given the opportunity to take each of the different 'hats' on different occasions and discuss which ones feel most comfortable to them personally. Some teachers provide actual hats for the children or cards with the different coloured hat on and examples of prompt questions.

 Classroom example

History, thinking skills

The children have been asked to imagine they are ancient Egyptian temple officials deciding how to organise the construction of a new temple building.

White hat:	*We've got lots of rock nearby but it needs to be cut to size and taken to the site and built up. We need people with different skills, some people to cut the rock, some to carry it, some to do the building.*
Green hat:	*Could we get slaves to do it?*

(Continued)

(Continued)

Yellow hat: *Well, we wouldn't have to pay them.*

Purple hat: *But all our slaves already work for other people, we'd have to go to war to capture some more to do the building.*

Red hat: *I don't think it's right to go to war just to get slaves to do our building.*

Yellow hat: *But it is a way of getting lots of workers.*

Red hat: *Yes, but …*

Blue hat: *Hang on a moment. Let's just think. What we need is people. We already have lots of people.*

Purple hat: *They're already busy.*

Green hat: *Not all the time. The farmers don't work when the river floods.*

Yellow hat: *They might be glad of the extra work if we gave them food.*

Red hat: *I'd feel better about using the farmers, they would get something and so would we.*

Purple hat: *But they haven't got the right skills.*

White hat: *Not all the jobs are skilled. They could move the stones.*

And so on …

Another useful strategy is something often called the 'Napoleon technique'. To do this you consider a problem from someone else's perspective. This could be a famous person with outstanding skills, so for example the children might consider how Gandhi would solve a particular problem. What skills and qualities would he bring to it? His solution would be compassionate, perhaps, offering insight and non-aggressive solutions, but he would not give way on the important principles. When the children have identified the particular characteristics their chosen hero would bring to bear on the problem, they can try to work out a solution that person might suggest.

Another way of considering a problem from different viewpoints is to use a number of different characters with different viewpoints or vested interests. So, for example, you might give the children role cards to consider the question of whether the school hall should be hired out at weekends for parties and dances. Roles might include a local resident in the same street, a local taxi firm, the school premises officer, the head teacher or a local DJ. Children might start by working in pairs with each role card and discussing what the pros and cons might be for each character before using that point of view to inform their discussion.

Being 'in the zone'

As was seen in Chapter 1, researchers in psychology and education have added considerably to our understanding of what makes a good learner. Part of that picture is of the learner 'locked into' their learning, totally absorbed, and if not unaware, uncaring of what is going on around them or how time is passing. This is what the psychologist Mihaly Csikszentmihalyi calls 'flow' (Csikszentmihalyi, 1990). In this state there is a 'buzz' about the challenge of learning, a real enjoyment of the feeling of being stretched. Guy Claxton, when writing about resilience in his book *Building Learning Power* (2002), divided resilience into four parts. These are absorption, managing distractions, noticing and perseverance. He makes the point that absorption does not have to be 'effortful concentration' (2002: 19) but can involve paying attention in a number of different ways, and he demonstrates the importance of 'attentive noticing: being able to identify the significant detail, or let an underlying pattern of connections emerge' (2002: 23).

One of the most useful classroom tools to aid developing absorption and noticing can be a hand-held magnifying glass. Even a cheap plastic lens can frame and concentrate an image and bring it forward to be noticed. This could be a map, a picture, the grain of a piece of wood or the spirals of a shell, but looking through a magnifying glass can make even the most distractible child concentrate.

Children who may not find the normal fare of the classroom overly absorbing are often the ones who respond best to outdoor learning, particularly in nature. Pond dipping, mini-beast observing, texture rubbing can be the type of activities that take some children into that state of intense interest and absorption.

It is worth using the opportunity to discuss how it feels to learn in those ways, for some children may not equate those activities with learning at all and may need help to highlight what they have in fact noticed, absorbed and processed during the activity. Similarly, some who may consider themselves poor learners may know a phenomenal amount about dinosaurs, certain computer games, or a 'cult' television programme. Paying attention to how much they know and asking how they learned it may help them recognise that they do indeed find learning in some areas so easy they are scarcely aware of it and then help them apply those skills to other areas.

In recent years there has been a growing interest in outdoor learning, with many schools investing in a long-term 'forest schools' curriculum of creative, open air, play-based activities. Organisations such as the Forest Schools Association (www.forestschoolsassociation.org), Learning Through Landscapes (www.ltl.org.uk/) or The Council for Learning Outside the Classroom (www.lotc.org.uk/) can offer advice on training and activities.

Chapter summary

To be able to work and learn creatively a child will need to possess a number of skills and dispositions. These include perseverance, breaking tasks into steps, evaluating, trial and improvement, generating ideas, working in a group, listening and responding, thinking in different spheres, being absorbed and noticing. These skills and dispositions can be learned and enhanced by giving overt attention to and discussing their attributes, modelling, and lots of practice. Children can then apply these skills to the knowledge and skills they gain in subject-specific areas in order to work and learn creatively in those domains.

 Personal thought and reflection

- Which kinds of learning that you have observed or experienced would you consider to be creative and which were not? What were the features of the creative learning?
- Which activities that have you observed in the classroom fostered learning or thinking skills?
- What are the personal attributes of children you consider to be creative learners? Do these differ from the attributes of children you would consider to be 'creative'?
- In which activities do you notice children being really absorbed? How does this apply to individuals in the class or classes you are observing?

 Individual activity

Look at a recent lesson plan (your own or someone else's) and identify the elements that required particular learning or thinking skills, e.g. persistence, discussion, generating ideas, working in a group.

How could you introduce, highlight or review these skills to enable children to make better use of them?

 Group activity

Share the outcomes of the individual activity and discuss the methods proposed. Are there any potential drawbacks to the changes to the lesson plans you have proposed? What are the advantages?

Further study

Critical reflection: Activity 3

Allow an hour for this activity.

This chapter has encouraged you to consider how you engage with children in order to develop their thinking and learning abilities. *Identify* the key areas discussed in this chapter.

Choose a sequence of lessons that you have taught in an area that interests you, for example five or six consecutive science lessons. *Identify* the key thinking and learning processes that you aimed to teach during those lessons.

Write these key points in two lists:

Table 3.1

Key areas discussed in the chapter	Key thinking and learning processes in my lessons

Observe and consider your two lists. Take time to reflect on what these say about your classroom practice.

Compare and contrast your lists. Ask yourself 'what if ... I taught ... differently by ... ?' Consider the possible consequences of making specific and particular changes to the teaching and learning processes in these lessons.

Write a brief *analysis* of what you have learnt from this thinking time. *Identify* any changes you want to try out in your classroom.

Speculate – what outcomes do you expect from these changes?

Further reading

Claxton, G. (2002) *Building Learning Power*. London: TLO.
Craft, A. (2005) *Creativity in Schools: Tensions and Dilemmas*. London: Routledge.
Society for Advancing Philosophical Enquiry and Reflection in Education (www.sapere.org.uk). This educational charity promotes philosophical enquiry for children.

CHAPTER 4

ESTABLISHING THE ETHOS

 Learning objectives in this chapter:

- To consider how a classroom ethos is established
- To consider the importance of the classroom layout and organisation
- To understand the importance of relationships, motivation and autonomy to learning creatively and learning to be creative

Relevant Teachers' Standards for this chapter

A teacher must:

1   Set high expectations which inspire, motivate and challenge pupils

1a   establish a safe and stimulating environment for pupils, rooted in mutual respect

1b   set goals that stretch and challenge pupils of all backgrounds, abilities and dispositions

1c   demonstrate consistently the positive attitudes, values and behaviour which are expected of pupils

2	**Promote good progress and outcomes by pupils**
2c	guide pupils to reflect on the progress they have made and their emerging needs
2e	encourage pupils to take a responsible and conscientious attitude to their own work and study
5	**Adapt teaching to respond to the strengths and needs of all pupils**
5b	have a secure understanding of how a range of factors can inhibit pupils' ability to learn, and how best to overcome these
5c	demonstrate an awareness of the physical, social and intellectual development of children, and know how to adapt teaching to support pupils' education at different stages of development
5d	have a clear understanding of the needs of all pupils, including those with special educational needs; those of high ability; those with English as an additional language; those with disabilities; and be able to use and evaluate distinctive teaching approaches to engage and support them
7	**Manage behaviour effectively to ensure a good and safe learning environment**
7a	have clear rules and routines for behaviour in classrooms, and take responsibility for promoting good and courteous behaviour both in classrooms and around the school, in accordance with the school's behaviour policy
7c	manage classes effectively, using approaches which are appropriate to pupils' needs in order to involve and motivate them

When you enter a school for the first time it is possible to gain an insight very quickly as to the sort of school it is: what the values and main aims are, what the expectations for the children's work and behaviour are, how the school fits within its local community. The same is true when you enter a classroom. These impressions are built up from what we see around us, what we hear, even what we smell, and they contribute to a range of emotions and feelings about the place. Does it excite us and stimulate us? Does it make us feel peaceful? Does it feel threatening or intimidating? Does it encourage us to want to shout or whisper, to run or walk carefully?

Those of us who want to teach have mostly had good experiences ourselves of being in school and so we are probably predisposed to feel comfortable in a school environment. This is not true of everyone, however, and many people, adults and children can feel nervous and intimidated in a school. No one can learn well in an environment where they do not feel comfortable, no one can experiment in a situation where they fear they will fail and be judged accordingly, no one will venture personal opinions where they believe they will be ridiculed. Daniel Goleman in his book *Emotional Intelligence* wrote, 'Students who are anxious, angry or depressed don't learn; people who are in these states do not take in information efficiently or deal with it well' (Goleman, 1995). Therefore creating a classroom ethos that encourages the aims, values and types of relationships that foster good learning is crucially important.

Individual or group activity

(Potential activity spoiler! Cover the paragraphs beneath this box.)

If you entered the most 'creative' classroom you can imagine what would you see and hear?

Use a large sheet of paper and big pens to record your ideas. This can be in words or pictures. Try to avoid jargon: instead of saying 'the children would be engaged' describe instead how you would know they are engaged, what they would be saying and doing.

This doesn't have to be at just one point in time.

If working in a group, share your ideas.

Many teachers find it quite hard to visualise exactly what they are aiming for, especially as practicalities such as the size and shape of your classroom, the attitudes of other staff or the nature of the actual class you have may colour what you believe to be possible. For now we should put to one side whether things are possible in a particular situation and concentrate on an ideal. Then we can see how close to that we can actually get.

Below is a selection of responses from teachers and students who have undertaken the above activity:

- Children moving around the room freely, collecting what they need by themselves.
- A hum of purposeful talk.
- Children working both in groups and individually.
- Children asking, 'Can I go to Green class and ask if I can borrow their empty fish tank?' 'What would happen if we froze it?'
- Children asking each other for advice.
- The teacher moving from group to group, sometimes watching and listening and taking notes, sometimes questioning.
- The teacher sometimes calling all the children together to discuss something that has come up, to ask for advice or opinions for a particular group, to share something that has been discovered, to move the activity on.
- Smiling, interested, puzzled faces.
- Children sitting in a circle discussing something.
- A group of children acting something out, the others watching and then asking them questions.
- Some children sitting or even lying down with books in a cushioned area.
- Children taking something they have made outside the room to test it.
- Children using laptops or tablets as they need them.

It is possible that you will be lucky enough to work in a school where these sorts of interactions are commonplace. In most schools the Early Years settings will function like this, however as learning becomes more formal and children get older a lively, enquiring classroom can become a thing of the past.

Taking time for personal and social learning

Establishing a classroom where a creative atmosphere persists takes time. It does not happen overnight, it needs reinforcing continually, and in a school where such values and methodology are not the norm, or in an environment where personal interactions may be more confrontational, it may only be possible to take small steps towards your ideal. Changes need to be gradual, positive and reinforced.

Feeling empowered to take the time to establish a classroom ethos where creative teaching and learning can flourish can be difficult. There are any number of pressures to 'cover' the curriculum, which will undoubtedly feel overcrowded, and succumbing to those pressures can lead to you feeling as if you are driving down a motorway at speed 'delivering' that curriculum by tossing snippets out of the window as you go. Taking the time to establish the relationships and attitudes that are necessary in order to learn well is time well spent, particularly at the beginning of the school year. What you establish then, if you can maintain it, will pay dividends later when the rate at which the children tackle new ideas and the depth at which they think can increase significantly.

One of the first things to establish is that each individual in the class feels valued, that their opinions will be listened to and they will be treated with respect.

It can be surprising how, even in a class that has been together for years, some children seem only to know the others in their 'set' and do not mix with or even know the names of all the children in their class. You may hear children talking about other class members as 'that girl'. So, don't make assumptions about an established class knowing each other well enough, or having seen through preconceptions or stereotypes that may have persisted for years.

 Classroom ideas

PSHE

- Take the time to play some 'finding out' games that establish similarities and shared interests. In a space that is big enough to move around safely, ask the children to find three other people who enjoy a particular computer game or have a pet or are the youngest in their family. Keep playing this over time with

(Continued)

(Continued)

different things to find out. After a couple of rounds ask the children to name others they found with things in common. If necessary, choose things that you know will involve them needing to interact with children they do not normally mix with. If there are some who are considered 'loners' or who are generally left out of the most dominant groups, you might discover some shared interests and be able to establish times when a carefully mixed group can bring in their games or hobby to play together. This could be during a lunchtime as a special treat for a specified period if you or someone else are prepared and able to supervise it.

- You could try taking photographs of the children and back them with hook-and-loop tape or magnetic strips and make similar labels with their names on. Challenge the children to see who can match all the photos and names in the quickest time or use them for the children to register themselves when they come in.
- Let the children know that you will be moving their groups and seating arrangements around often so that they work with different people and that you set store by how well they can do this. Spend time discussing the attributes of good cooperation, make them learning objectives alongside your subject-specific objectives, and evaluate how well these were achieved.
- Use a jar of marbles for a whole class cumulative reward system. This can be very motivating. Put an empty jar or vase in the classroom. If you see or hear a child doing something helpful or kind for another then put a marble in the jar. This works best if you do not tell the children what you are doing, and if they ask what the jar is for then just be mysterious and say, 'That's for you to find out.' When they do finally work this out, praise them for their discovery and explain that when the jar is full there will be a reward for the whole class. It can be nice to ask the children to nominate what sort of rewards they would appreciate (subject to whether there are funds available of course), but most classes will be quite happy with an hour watching a DVD with popcorn or a trip to the park to play frisbee.

Many teachers will spend time at the beginning of the year establishing a class charter, a coat of arms or class banner. There are many good activities in the 'New Beginnings' lesson opportunities in the SEAL materials (DfES, 2005). One of those ideas is to create a class totem pole with each individual contributing a model or drawing to represent something that is special to them or represents them as an individual. As in the coat of arms or class banner these images are used compositely to represent the whole class. The totem pole or banner can be referred back to, to emphasise the fact that the class is a unit made up of all the individuals in it. It is important to emphasise to the children that they all have skills to offer in class.

Classroom example

PSHE

A teacher of a class of 7 and 8 year olds was aware that some children, particularly those on the autistic spectrum, had particular skills that were overlooked by others. She said to the class that she had noticed she was teaching a class of superheroes who each had special abilities in different areas. She wanted to set up a register of their special abilities so that when other people were in need of help they knew who to call on.

The children drew pictures of themselves in their secret superhero identities and costumes and then listed their special abilities. These covered a huge range including being good at football, drawing or spelling, speaking another language, being good at helping people sort out arguments, computer skills, map reading, looking after pets or plants, singing, being good with younger children and so on.

The teacher displayed the list in the classroom and encouraged the children to use it to choose classmates to help them when necessary, to offer coaching at playtimes, and she created opportunities for all the children to use their special skills around the school and have them recognised.

Alongside the children feeling comfortable with each other and confident in their abilities it is important that there is an atmosphere that will help promote creative thought. In previous chapters the need to be a 'risk-taker' was introduced and the idea that creative ideas are often unconventional. Children tend to want to be 'one of the crowd' at school, not to stand out and certainly not to put themselves in a situation where they might be ridiculed.

As teachers it is important we do not underestimate the complexity of the messages we give to children in the classroom. There are times when we expect everyone to conform; we cannot allow individuals to opt out when we need everyone to line up for assembly or come and sit down on the carpet. We need times when they all listen to us or to another child and know not to interrupt. There are other times, however, when we want each child to operate as an individual, when we want them to come up with a totally original idea for a story or a painting for example. Most children absorb these different demands on them seamlessly and learn to respond appropriately in different situations. There are, however, some children who do not understand the different 'rules' that apply and they will need us to be overt in our explanations of how they should behave: 'This is a time when I need you all to do exactly the same thing' or 'When you do this I'm looking to see how many really different ideas you can come up with.'

Classroom idea

Learning skills

It can help to encourage children to be free with their ideas to have times when you accept contributions that are really 'off the wall'. This could be a feature of an odd five minutes at the beginning or end of a session.

Try asking children to describe or draw on the board the weirdest clock they can imagine, or the most peculiar hairstyle, or the funniest-looking alien. In this situation children are generally happy to come up with wild and wacky ideas and you can even ask them to 'judge' their 'wacky rating' by holding up a number of fingers out of ten. Most children will be pleased if their idea causes others to laugh. More eccentric ideas will become acceptable and the children more used to trying to come up with something out of the ordinary.

If you do get times when some children are making unkind comments or laughing inappropriately then this needs dealing with fully. Merely telling the children off or having a 'no put downs' poster on the wall is not going to be enough. Ask calmly why they are laughing or making comments. Tell them they do not have to agree with other people's ideas and contributions but the widest collection of ideas and contributions helps everyone to sort out what they think and feel. Start a session when children are going to be asked to contribute ideas or comments by reminding them 'This is an all-contributions-gratefully-received session, so listen carefully to other people's ideas and think in your head whether their idea is useful to you. Keep an open mind because sometimes ideas that sound a bit strange or even stupid can be the ones that are really original and useful.' For more ideas on how to encourage appropriate behaviour the chapter 'Creative approaches to behaviour management' in *Effective Behaviour Management in the Primary Classroom* (Shelton and Brownhill, 2008) might prove useful.

Classroom layout and environment

The physical environment that you and the children are in will have a great deal of influence over how they interact and learn. Setting up your classroom is likely to be a matter of compromise as a classroom that is large enough to fulfil all the functions you would ideally want is a rarity indeed. There are, however, many factors over which you have control which can help or hinder the development of creative teaching and learning.

Probably the most fundamental feature is how you place your tables and chairs. Do you have rows or groups? Is the whiteboard the focus? Is there a carpet area where children can sit up close to you and each other? Ideally you will want as much flexibility as possible and the option to adapt seating arrangements when necessary. A default arrangement where children sit in groups but can easily turn their chairs to see the board is probably preferable.

Encouraging good group work is fundamental to creative, enquiry-based learning and group seating needs to encourage cooperation and collaboration. If the tables are too big then children can't hear each other well or see resources they might be using. Children quickly lose concentration if they can only see something upside down or not clearly enough because the resource is on the far side of a large table. If you know children will be working in groups for a concentrated period, then sitting six children round a table that is normally for four, or three at a table for two, can give better results.

A carpet area, even for older children, can be very useful. The whole class can sit together to share a story or discussion without people having to project their voices so much and it provides a 'soft' area for reading or individual or paired work, particularly if there are cushions. Some children can find it very hard to sit at a table for any length of time and the option to take work to the carpet and be able to sit and work more informally can be very helpful.

 Personal thought and reflection

Think about how you work or study best. Do you always sit at a table? Do you ever have your laptop on your lap, lie on the sofa or sit in the garden? Are there ways you can offer some variety to where and how children sit in the classroom?

 Individual activity

Think about different classroom layouts you have observed. How did they influence the way teachers and pupils interacted? Were there certain activities that were difficult or would have been so in a particular classroom?

Ideally a classroom will have a number of areas where different types of activities can be carried out but in practice this can be very difficult to achieve. In encouraging creativity within the classroom, spaces where children can reflect and where they can experiment are really useful. You will also need storage space for work-in-progress. Space for reflection and quiet thought can, of course, double as a reading area or be the carpet area. If there is a sink area this can be a useful focus for experimentation with easily available construction kits, craft materials, individual whiteboards for trying out ideas or calculations, and storage shelves and drawers for children's projects as well as materials.

To encourage the use of different areas, particularly at first, it can be useful and fun to 'theme' the area and really focus on its use. Why not have white coats available in your 'exploration area'? Even the most sophisticated-seeming 11 year old can actually like dressing up and the hint of it being a role-play area can encourage its good use with any age of child. Spend time commenting positively on how you have observed individuals using particular areas well and talking to them about how useful an activity was. This will help other children see the possibilities for working in different ways.

Displays in these areas and all around the classroom are also important. Remember, however, that these do need to be changed regularly or they become merely 'wallpaper' and are not really looked at. This can be time-consuming but it is possible and very worthwhile to involve the children in designing the nature of the displays. In a classroom where creativity is valued, displays are going to enhance a problem-solving and investigative approach. There may well be posters designed by the children to remind them of possible ways forward if they get stuck or ways of approaching particular types of investigation. There could also be suggestion or question boxes in which children can post individual comments.

 Classroom idea

Learning skills

One of the most useful display ideas is to have a working wall. At its best, a working wall is a physical version of a Web forum where people can post ideas, comments and questions, and make links between what different individuals are doing. To make a working wall a positive contribution to learning it needs time spent daily focusing on what is on there, discussing how it is being used, and making suggestions for its potential use.

Ideas for uses

- The teacher or children can post questions about a particular topic.
- The teacher or children can post answers or suggestions in a 'thread'.
- Children can post draft pieces of work for others to comment on and give them suggestions.
- The teacher can make links between certain ideas, questions or pieces of work, and suggest collaborations or ways forward.
- Anyone (even parents or other staff) can post relevant pictures, articles or printouts, or suggested useful web addresses.

A working wall will be a work-in-progress and so, by its nature, a bit rough and untidy, but it is a wonderful way to exemplify the creative process.

Make sure this is at a height that the children can reach themselves. Have lots of sticky notes available. Try to add or change something every night after the children have left so they are excited next morning to see if there are new ideas, suggestions or feedback comments. Refer to the wall frequently and suggest to the class that they should post thoughts you have heard them voice. Use it and keep it fresh.

Making the room an attractive and interesting place to enter makes the activities that happen there special too. You could decorate the entrance to the room appropriately to represent the theme being studied, from a simple sign like 'School of Journalism' to a 3D rock formation (made of paper) that makes the doorway the entrance to a cave. Book corners can be similarly themed and if you are allowed to hang things from the ceiling your whole classroom could become a rainforest or a bug's-eye-view garden. If you want children to investigate then have microscopes or magnifying glasses out and change the range of things they can look at often as well as encourage them to bring in objects they have found. Encourage them also to sketch or note down descriptions of what they observe and you could even supply voice recorders for them to speak their observations. For more ideas on classroom organisation the chapter 'Organising your classroom for learning' in *Learning to Teach in the Primary School* (Arthur and Cremin, 2010) might prove useful.

 Classroom idea

Learning skills

It might be possible to utilise a little-used room, large cupboard or other space in school as a 'Wonder Room' or 'cabinet of curiosity'. Schools often have delightful collections of artefacts ranging from ancient household objects to fossils and natural found objects. These can be fascinating to children and the starting place for many investigations. Often teachers will only use these when they bring them into the classroom to link up with a particular 'topic', but taking the children to or allowing small groups to visit an area outside their classroom just to explore such objects can be enormously stimulating to their curiosity. For more information try searching 'school wonder room' on the internet, or for inspiration dip into the charming *The Little Book of Awe and Wonder: A Cabinet of Curiosities* (McFall, 2013). Perhaps your class could collect and curate their own version.

Pupil voice

During the 1990s there were considerable advances in the extent that children and young people were encouraged to participate in matters that concerned them. These were enshrined internationally in the 1989 UN Convention on the Rights of the Child, and in UK education policy in Every Child Matters in 2003 and the Children's Act in 2004. As well as fundamental changes in children's services, one of the outcomes of these developments was increased interest in the role that children should and could take in their education.

Professor Jean Rudduck, in her discussion article 'Pupil voice is here to stay!' (Rudduck, 2005), points to four generalised 'pupil states'. She identifies the 'positive-active' pupil as one who 'wants to understand and contribute, wants to discuss progress in learning, is ready to organise things and take responsibility and is ready to help other pupils' (2005: 1). These are definitely attributes of a creative learner and Rudduck's article and others demonstrate the positive outcomes both socially and for learning when children are consulted and given a measure of autonomy in the classroom and beyond.

Many teachers are now consulting children about what they want to learn. Often the particular themes and topics within different subjects are already prescribed by school planning so this can appear tokenistic, but there is still scope for children to have quite an input. (For detailed consideration about the possibilities and potential for planning creatively and for creativity see Chapters 7, 8 and 9.) If you really want to use children's ideas and interests in your planning be sure to allow enough time to be able to find resources and do your own research if necessary. Discussing the following term at the end of the previous one allows you sufficient time to be prepared. Children, when asked what they want to learn or know about Ancient Egypt, for example, are often liable to tell you what they know previous year groups have studied before them. It is often better to ascertain what they already know and then have a discussion where you ask probing questions such as 'Why do you think they did that?', 'What do you think people in Europe were doing at the same time?', 'Why do you think they believed in lots of gods?', 'Do you believe in magic?' Discussing these issues will hopefully whet their appetite to explore other issues that come up. These can be noted down for future research, use in a community of enquiry, or for other sorts of exploration. Once you have begun work on the topic any new issues that emerge can be noted on the working wall or new questions posed to excite their curiosity.

Be alert for children's interests all the time though. If something comes up that you do not have the time or resources to deal with straightaway, record this on a piece of paper and tell the children you are very interested in pursuing this idea and will do so at a specified point in the future and they should remind you about it. Put the piece of paper where everyone can see it until you are able to deal with it.

Another way of giving children more autonomy over their learning is to present them with more choices with regard to how they will tackle a task. Firstly, think about the resources the children will need. It has become the fashion over the last couple of decades to put everything the class will need on the table for them in order that they do not 'wander' about the room and waste time or irritate other children. It is not unusual to hear head teachers telling teachers not to let children leave their seats without asking permission. Granted, it is understandable how much simpler this is for the teacher and how it can cut down on disruption – but there is another side to this. If children are never allowed to move around the room freely, then they will not develop the interpersonal skills that mean they can function in a crowded space without causing friction or inconvenience; if everything is provided for the children they will quickly cease to think for themselves which tools might be necessary for the task in hand and they are far more likely to produce identical pieces of work to everyone else if they all use identical formats. If you observe a group of 3 and 4 year olds they will almost certainly be self-motivated, moving freely, collecting whatever they need for a task, asking if they need something they cannot find, and competently resourcing themselves. Why then should older children not be able to do the same? So try putting classroom equipment in clearly marked accessible places and encourage the class to use these. It will take time for them to learn how to do this sensibly if they are not used to it, but it will make them far more able to work independently.

A second thing to consider is the task itself. Many teachers will specify exactly how something is to be done, whether it is how something should be set out on paper or how a model is to be made. This does ensure the results are likely to be competent for every child but reduces any creative input into the task, except perhaps the decoration. How often have you observed whole classes going home with identical Mother's Day cards or Ancient Greek clay pots? Some schools have even made this uniformity of outcome a policy as parents may complain if some children have different outcomes. However, parents will generally understand completely if the reasons for children doing individual work are explained to them. As far as a creative task is concerned, it is very possible to teach the particular skills you want the children to use and then give them the freedom and flexibility as to how they apply these. So, for example, if in Design and Technology you have explored the uses for hinges or pop-ups or sliders the children themselves could apply those features to an entirely individual product. They will also need guidance in reflecting on their own progress and ongoing learning needs and help in taking responsibility for their own learning and outcomes. For teachers there will be a balance between accepting what the children can produce independently, challenging them to achieve more highly, and helping them produce outcomes they can be proud of.

Creativity and specific learning needs

Much of what has already been written in this and preceding chapters relates strongly to addressing the needs of children as individuals and when teaching children with different learning needs the same thought processes pertain. The classroom ethos of accepting individuals' needs, strengths and qualities is crucial here. Differences may make it harder for some children to learn in particular ways but give them strengths in other areas.

In the autumn of 2014 it was revealed in the press that GCHQ made a point of employing analysts and code breakers with dyslexia and dyspraxia, as these 'neuro-diverse' individuals were often outstandingly good at seeing patterns or making connections and their 3D spatial-perception awareness may be particularly good or their creativity in problem solving better than average. (See the articles in various news websites for 21st September 2014.) This was a salutary reminder to us to plan to enable all children to learn and demonstrate that learning.

One thing we can be sure to do is to encourage diverse ways for children to demonstrate what they know and have learned. The use of video recording, pictures, models, presentations etc. can show us as much and more than a piece of writing. As we try to make the classroom a place that accepts individuals' needs we can be sure to offer opportunities to work in ways that will suit the individual. Therefore, an ethos that accepts that not everyone will work in exactly the same way on exactly the same piece of work at exactly the same time can be extremely helpful.

We can try to engage children by building work around particular interests. For example, a child with autism who has particular 'obsessions' can start with work built around this area, and then the teacher can try to encourage avenues that will widen the scope step by step. We can also try to find time within each half term for children to follow their interests and undertake their own inquiries, supported by their teacher. Children can be encouraged to prepare and 'pitch' a project idea, and if successful, can be given the time to pursue it.

Understanding the needs of individuals by talking to them, their parents, and previous teachers and support workers, and observing them carefully to discover what helps them learn well and be comfortable in the classroom, is really important. Sometimes catering for individual needs in a busy classroom can be very difficult to achieve but understanding and creative problem solving on your part will often be able to provide solutions that work. For example, you will want bright and stimulating displays in the classroom but some children with autism can find this over-stimulating. If that is the case you could make one side of the classroom a visually 'quiet' side and sit children who find this preferable facing that side of the room. Making smaller calm areas with screens can also help children who find too much movement and 'buzz' distracting.

Changes to routine and flexibility are often features of a creative classroom but can prove difficult for some children. Try to let them know in advance if there are going to be changes to the routine, thereby giving them time to take on board what the changes will mean to them and to mentally adapt. The use of visual timetables at the start of each day with symbols and pictures to represent the different activities can help children with a number of different learning needs.

A good starting place for more information might be *Teaching Primary Special Educational Needs* (Glazzard et al., 2010).

Types of interactions

As we have seen, and will develop in subsequent chapters, being a creative teacher and encouraging creativity in the children we teach will mean spending less time in 'transmission' mode, i.e. telling children information, and more time in facilitating enquiry, investigation and children drawing their own conclusions. This involves different types of interactions between teacher and pupil, and like other methods of working will have to be practised in order for them to become the way the class naturally functions.

We have already looked at the importance of open-minded attitudes and children being confident to venture opinions and disagree amicably. Children also need to embrace the mindset that there are not necessarily right and wrong answers to everything. Some things are clear-cut and factual but others are matters of opinion. Teachers often require children to respond extraordinarily quickly to questions and will move on to other children if they do not get a speedy response. If we want considered opinions we have to be prepared to take a little longer but also use methods that will still maintain children's interest and involvement.

 Classroom ideas

Learning skills

- After asking a question encourage children to discuss this with 'talk partners' so that everyone has had a chance to voice their opinion before you ask them to share the outcomes.
- Notify children of any questions you want them to consider for the next day so they can come prepared.
- Allow them the chance to say 'Can I come back to that?' Move on but make sure you do return to the question later.
- Encourage a genuine 'I'm not sure' as being an acceptable answer, but then ask the child to listen to other responses and to say later which of these they would tend to support and why.

Children also need to be given time to plan, to develop ideas, and to evaluate what they are doing or what they have done.

Adult involvement

One of the most important things to establish with children is that learning is something that everyone can enjoy and appreciate and that can and should continue all of our life. In order to do this you would need to establish a climate where adults sharing what they are learning becomes a regular occurrence in your classroom.

Being a role model yourself as a learner is vital and in the next chapter we will examine this at some length, but you should also try to involve other adults. Do the teaching assistants have hobbies that they find they get better at as they work at them? Perhaps they could share their experiences of fitness or hobbies, or bring in crafts that they could demonstrate to the children, and then talk about what they find easy, what can be hard or frustrating, how much they are improving. Parents too may be able to come in and share their learning experiences. Children learn well by being 'apprentices' to adults who have a particular skill. Many schools are lucky enough to have times where they have an artist in residence and children can work alongside them and learn how they perform their specialism. If your school is not part of such a scheme, then perhaps you know someone who has skills in a particular area who would be prepared to spend some time in school, perhaps an hour a week for a few weeks. They do not have to 'teach' the class but be prepared for the children to watch them working and answer questions. They might be painters, practise a craft, be expert gardeners or sports people. Classrooms in schools can all too easily become worlds that only teachers and their classes inhabit, and so bringing other people in and showing how they work, learn and develop can be really inspiring and motivating for children.

Chapter summary

In this chapter we have seen how important it is to establish practices, interactions and an environment where children will feel empowered and comfortable. To be creative involves risk, and children need to be able to trust their teacher and classmates to respond to their ideas and contributions positively. The classroom itself needs to be set out to encourage the sort of investigative work that will be going on, and be flexible enough to support individual and group work in a variety of situations. Children need to be treated as individuals, encouraged to develop responsibility for their own learning, and be given a measure of autonomy to make decisions about what and how they learn. They also need good role models of adults as learners.

 Personal thought and reflection

Go back to your visualisation of a highly creative classroom. Which of the features that you imagined have you seen in action in a real classroom? Which of the features that have been outlined in this chapter have you seen in action in a real classroom? What features can you now imagine in a classroom where you were the teacher? Close your eyes if it helps and visualise yourself showing a visitor around your classroom where the children are all working productively. How would you describe what is important to you? How would you point out the importance of different areas in the room and how you like to work with the children? Return to this visualisation from time to time and add detail; 'dream' the conversations you might have with the children and how you might welcome them in the morning, or what you might do in the room after they have left at night.

 Further study
Critical Reflection: Activity 4

Allow an hour for this activity.

This chapter has encouraged you to consider how you provide a creative environment where interactions between children take place to enhance learning. *Evaluate* on a 0–10 scale where you are on the journey to provide an engaging environment where children have a voice that is respected:

0--10 (most creative, engaging)

Identify the evidence that suggests that you are at this stage. *Analyse* this evidence. For example: in a few sentences consider what you have planned to provide within the learning environment, how you support the environment, what effects this provision has had on children's learning.

What aspect would you be motivated to improve? What do you need to do to make this improvement? Where would you aim to be on this journey (0–10) in three months' time?

Is there anything preventing/hindering you from taking the next step to this progress? Can you come up with a solution to this hindrance? If not, perhaps you could discuss this with a trusted colleague/mentor.

📖 Further reading

Dean, J. (2008) *Organising Learning in the Primary School Classroom*, 4th edn. London: Routledge.

McFall, M. (2013) *The Little Book of Awe and Wonder: A Cabinet of Curiosities*. Carmarthen: Independent Thinking Press, an imprint of Crown House Publishing.

Rudduck, J. (2005) 'Pupil voice is here to stay!', *QCA Futures – Meeting the Challenge*. London: QCA Online publication.

Shelton, F. and Brownhill, S. (2008) *Effective Behaviour Management in the Primary Classroom*. Maidenhead: Open University Press.

PART 3

A CREATIVE TEACHER

This section concentrates on you as a teacher. It looks at the skills and attributes you will need both to teach creatively and encourage the development of creativity in your pupils. You will be encouraged to consider your own creativity in whatever way it may manifest itself, as examining our own creativity can lead us to understand better the creativity of the children we teach. We will consider the difficult realities of time management and how to manage a flexible approach within a structured and secure learning environment. A successful creative teacher will have good subject knowledge and a strong core identity as a teacher, and we will examine the development of these attributes. Certain skills that are useful to the creative teacher are also looked at in more depth, including facilitating, questioning, using a sketchbook/scrapbook approach, motivating, and using drama techniques.

CHAPTER 5

WHAT MAKES A CREATIVE TEACHER?

 Learning objectives in this chapter:

To understand the key knowledge, skills and interactions that a teacher needs to teach effectively both creatively and to foster creativity, including:

- To model creative working processes yourself
- To be able to identify creativity in others
- To be able to foster creativity in others
- To be able to encourage creativity in others
- To have and enhance the personal attributes that enable you to identify, foster and encourage creativity in others
- To identify and foster in yourself the pedagogic skills necessary to identify, foster and encourage creativity in others

Relevant Teachers' Standards for this chapter

A teacher must:

1   **Set high expectations which inspire, motivate and challenge pupils**

1c   demonstrate consistently the positive attitudes, values and behaviour which are expected of pupils

(Continued)

(Continued)

3   Demonstrate good subject and curriculum knowledge

3b   demonstrate a critical understanding of developments in the subject and curriculum areas, and promote the value of scholarship

4   Plan and teach well structured lessons

4b   promote a love of learning and children's intellectual curiosity

Many teachers claim that they themselves are not creative. They sincerely believe this but what they usually mean is that they are not talented in the arts. In the preceding chapters we have seen that to be creative is far wider than having talents and expertise in arts subjects and that creativity is a human characteristic we all share, although it will manifest itself in different ways in all of us.

The importance of your own creativity

Understanding your own creativity and being prepared to model your own creative working processes with the children is one of the cornerstones of helping them to recognise and make the most of their own creativity.

 Personal thought and reflection

In what ways are you creative? You began this process in Chapter 1. After what you have read so far can you identify more areas in which you could consider yourself to be creative?
   Think about:

- tactics in team games: are you a creative playmaker?
- cooking;
- designing (invitations, displays, home décor, fashion);
- music (playing or singing yourself, or maybe you can put together amazing playlists);
- photography;
- computer solutions;
- finding personal solutions for your own or others' problems;
- solving or working on puzzles, logic problems, patterns and sequences;
- choosing just the right present for people.

This is just the start of the list of possibilities. How many other areas can you identify and how many of them would you place yourself in? You might even want to score yourself on a scale of 0–10 and identify the areas where you consider yourself most or least creative. Are there areas where you have potential but could do more to develop?

Sharing and modelling your own creativity can take many forms. We have already discussed how teachers can 'speak aloud' their thought processes in terms of decision making and assessing alternative courses of action. If you have skills as, for example, an artist, dancer, gymnast or musician, then would you be prepared to share that expertise with the children? You might explain and explore the way you work and the choices you take. Why did you decide to take some photographs in black and white rather than colour? What difference did it make? How could you play a piece of music differently? How much scope is there for interpreting a composition in terms of tempo, ornamentation or dynamics? This is closely allied to modelling the learning process yourself.

Guy Claxton comments, 'One of the problems with conventional schooling is that it delivers knowledge to the students after all the interesting learning has taken place, and all the uncertainty, disagreement and trial-and-error has been squeezed out of it' (Claxton, 2002: 97). He goes on to suggest that children would learn better if they could see all the first drafts or initial observations that went into the works of art or scientific and mathematical theories they study. Teachers can help here. If you write poetry or songs or stories why not show your class the multiple drafts you generate before you are satisfied? Guy Claxton suggests teachers could set up their own science experiment in the classroom and talk through what they are trying to do. Perhaps you are involved in a mini action-research project, maybe about the children's learning, and could share your thinking and research methods. The possibilities are endless. The process need not take long but making sharing of that type a regular feature of your classroom will really help the children to see what a creative person and a successful learner does. You do not have to be an expert in order to do this, in fact it may inhibit the class if they are overawed by your prowess. Just showing your interest, enthusiasm and process is enough.

Identifying creativity

The NACCCE (1999) report identified three different tasks in teaching for creativity: identifying, encouraging and fostering. As we examine these three elements it is important to apply these to your own creativity as well as to that of the children you teach.

When you tried to identify in the activity above how you yourself were creative, you began by looking at particular domains such as photography or music, for as we have seen creativity expresses itself through such domains and you cannot be creative in a vacuum. However, certain personality characteristics have been identified by various research projects which can be viewed as characteristic of creative individuals. These are quoted by Anna Craft in her book *Creativity in Schools: Tensions and Dilemmas* (Craft, 2005: 56, 57) and are reproduced here:

- Achievement within a domain of knowledge.
- Seeking of order.
- Curiosity.

- Assertive, self-sufficient, dominant or even aggressive.
- Tendency to be less formal, less conventional, to reject repression and be less inhibited.
- Tendency to like work, to be self-disciplined and to be persistent.
- Independence and autonomy.
- Capacity to be constructively critical.
- Tendency to be widely informed.
- Openness to emotions and feelings.
- Personal judgement influenced by the aesthetic dimension.
- Capacity to adopt values that fit with the wider environment.
- Capacity to manifest masculine interests if female and vice versa if male without inhibition.
- Tendency not to require social interaction.
- Self-fulfilled and self-realised.

The above list was collated by Stein (1974) and the following by Torrance (1965):

- Having the courage to hold a strong opinion.
- Curiosity and search approach.
- Independent judgement.
- Intuition.
- Capacity to become preoccupied with tasks.
- Unwilling to accept things without being convinced with evidence.
- Idealistic and visionary.
- Risk-taking approach.

And Anna Craft added her own list:

- Goal directedness.
- Fascination for a task.
- Orientation toward risk-taking.
- Preference for asymmetry and complexity.
- Willingness to ask many (unusual) questions.
- Capacity to display results and consult other people.
- A desire to go beyond the conventional.

Obviously a creative individual would not display all of the above characteristics and some might seem contradictory, but looking out for these characteristics in others can help you identify where creativity is manifesting itself. It is also evident that some of the characteristics are those that will not necessarily endear you to others or make you easy to get on with. As teachers we will have to foster creativity but also help individuals to handle their personality traits in socially acceptable ways without stifling their individuality.

Personal thought and reflection

Think about people you know or have known whom you consider to be creative. This might be friends, family, colleagues, or children you have taught. Which of the above personality characteristics do they exhibit? Have these characteristics caused them any problems with relationships? If so, was this more likely with peers or with authority? Have these individuals had to make changes to accommodate others or do other people tend to accommodate them?

Teachers need to be able to identify creativity in many different situations. Christopher Bannerman (2008), writing on 'Creativity and wisdom', reminds us that these creative expressions might be 'vibrant and overt, or secret and personal' and perhaps appear completely unexpectedly. He cites the example of 'individuals experiencing a sudden unleashing of creative energies, which appeared to be entirely hidden previously, through contact with a new context or discipline' (Bannerman, 2008: 140). Most, if not all, teachers will have recognised this phenomenon. It most often happens when a child is working with an outside agency visiting the school or a learning experience outside the classroom. Unusual working methods, different relationships with the teacher/facilitator and a different setting can seem to stimulate responses in some children which are unexpected and surprising. When this happens and a teacher notices the engagement they can then find ways to encourage and foster that spark of creativity in the future.

Encouraging and fostering creativity

For a teacher in regular contact with their class, and with more established and necessary practices and procedures, it can be harder to provide experiences that will allow for expressions of creativity to be stimulated than would be the case for an outside facilitator. A creative teacher needs to steer a steady course through their days and weeks. They will need to balance structure and security in regular classroom procedures with innovation and flexibility. This can be difficult to achieve, particularly in the early stages of a teaching career, and teachers should give themselves space and time to develop the skills and confidence they will need and to develop within the children they teach the skills and confidence to work in this way. It should be a slow and steady process for all parties.

Classroom idea

Teaching skills

To help children feel comfortable and confident in working in different ways, be sure to make very clear to them exactly what your expectations are: 'In this activity I want you to move around and talk to as many people as you can until I ring the bell', or 'In this activity I want you to sit still and quietly in your seats and think the problem through on your own before we share our ideas.' If you clarify the type of activity and your expectations of behaviour during that activity the class will not find you inconsistent and will be secure in what is required. You may, of course, have to stop them and reinforce sensible behaviour and working practices until they are used to working in a range of different ways, but if you are consistent in doing so they will soon respond.

A creative teacher needs to be comfortable with flexibility and able to change routines where appropriate. However, flexibility leads to uncertainty and this is an integral part of creativity. 'Problem-solving at all levels requires people to face uncertainty' says Leslie Safran, 'to be open to all sorts of solutions and to be uncertain about the answers they are looking for' (Safran, 2001: 88). Some people are much happier about open-ended activities than others, and as a teacher you will have to balance the need to address certain areas of learning and to plan for particular outcomes while allowing (or even planning for) the unexpected to happen.

 Classroom idea

Teaching skills

Begin by planning for expected outcomes. Have a clear 'route' that you want the lesson to take, and take notice when children suggest ideas, solutions or different avenues that you had not anticipated when you planned. Record these on paper and commend the children for their responses. Say you will come back to these ideas in subsequent lessons but for now you want to pursue a particular route. Display the ideas on your 'working wall' or noticeboard, and plan ways to address these in the future.

Once you are comfortable that you can plan lessons that go where you want them to and fulfil the objectives you planned for, you can then try planning a more open-ended activity where you are less sure of the outcomes.

You may also want to take advantage of the unexpected stimulus that can appear in school: a windy or snowy day, something a child has brought in, an occurrence in the news, the ceiling suddenly leaking. In these situations you will have to make decisions quickly as to the educational value they will offer. It might simply be that the excitement they generate gives children the motivation to create good descriptive phrases to use in their writing, and going out to experience the weather, or touching and looking at shells or a bird's nest, can prove an immediate stimulus that engages them. In changing the direction of your English lesson it will be quite easy to substitute the learning objectives you will achieve from this activity for what you had planned. You will later on have to find an opportunity for your original learning objectives to be achieved. Sometimes, though, the potential of an unexpected stimulus might impact on more than one lesson. What if the leaking roof leads to a whole possible investigation into waterproof materials, water containers and materials that absorb liquid, or the bird's nest to questions about flight and feathers and wind resistance or insulation? Here you will have to make more difficult decisions. You will need to think about the following questions:

- Are these areas that would have been on the curriculum this year anyway?
- Have the children already had experience in learning in these areas? Or will they in the future?
- Which generic skills will be generated (e.g. research skills, using the internet or non-fiction books; close observational drawing)?

If you can identify areas of the curriculum that you would have covered in other ways at a different time during the year, then addressing them now while the children's interest is excited might be a very sensible thing to do. If they have already addressed learning in that area you could build on what they have already learned, reminding them of past learning, making connections, and extending their thinking by applying it in new circumstances. If you identify generic skills that can be addressed now in an authentic situation rather than creating a situation for them at another time, that is obviously worthwhile too. The most difficult situation is likely to be launching into studying, for example waterproof materials and absorbency, when you know they would cover this next year. Your decision in that case will have much to do with how the school works and your relationship with other teachers. Many would be happy to know what prior experience the children have had, will assess what they already know, and understand and tailor what they teach accordingly. We will look more closely at the planning process in such cases in subsequent chapters, but it will be seen that in encouraging creativity a creative teacher must balance being able to recognise the potential for enquiry, and take advantage of the moment the children are motivated to learn in a particular area, with their responsibility for teaching certain curriculum areas during the school year.

Making these kinds of decisions requires a teacher to have good subject knowledge in the whole range of National Curriculum subjects. They will need to understand the progression of skills inherent in each subject and the range and breadth of the areas of learning. They will also need to have enough confidence in what they are teaching to be able to be flexible. As Margaret Boden, writing on 'Creativity and knowledge' (2001: 101) says, 'The teacher who lacks the relevant knowledge, who thinks in rigidly prescribed fashions, who cannot try to make their intuitions explicit and who lacks the self-confidence to say "Let's try this!" or "I don't know" will feel helpless and threatened if asked to teach in the ways sketched above'. She outlines three different types of creative thinking: combinational, exploratory, and trans-formational. As their names imply these correlate with the key elements of creativity outlined in Chapter 1 of this book. Boden makes the point that all these types of creative thinking are 'grounded in previous knowledge, but the way this knowledge is used differs in each case. It follows that the way to encourage them – or to smother them – differs too' (2001: 96).

Combinational creativity refers to combining ideas in different or unex-pected ways, and Boden makes the point that in order to do this a person needs a rich 'memory bank' of ideas to use and the confidence to apply them: 'The more diverse types of knowledge (concepts, not just "facts") a person acquires, the richer their mental source for making novel combina-tions of ideas' (2001: 96). So, in order to encourage this type of creativity a teacher has to provide a broad and rich curriculum and encourage their class to enjoy and use the knowledge they have acquired. It also helps if children experience knowledge without it being rigidly compartmentalised.

 Classroom ideas

Thinking skills, English

- Put words in a hat and ask the children to draw out two. They should then find a way to combine the two words, perhaps by putting them both into a sentence or stating three ways in which they are similar and three ways in which they are different.
- Enjoy and analyse puns and jokes that rely on word play. Use homonyms and homophones to create jokes: e.g. 'When is a door not a door? When it's ajar.'

(Adapted from Boden, 2001: 100)

Exploratory creativity assumes that a person has learned a certain amount in a particular domain and can then explore or 'play around' with the 'rules' or ideas. This might take the form of a musician improvising on a particular chord sequence or a mathematician using knowledge in one area to prove something else. Again we must meet the need to allow children the time to explore ideas in different areas, to challenge them with 'what would happen if … ?', and encourage them to ask that of themselves. It needs to be acceptable to try these approaches even if it turns out there is nothing to be gained. Blind alleys teach us where there are blind alleys and that this is knowledge gained, just as much as finding a route to something new and exciting.

Sometimes exploratory creativity may lead directly to transformational creativity where the 'rules' of a domain are changed or seen to be different. This is the type of creativity that leads to new inventions or discoveries. Transformational creativity will always break some of the norms or 'rules' of a domain. Think of the proof that the earth was a sphere, or the theory of evolution, and how these ideas shocked established thought and beliefs; how abstract painting shattered accepted ideas about representation. When established rules are broken many people will deny the value of the new idea and it is genuinely difficult to establish whether a revolutionary idea or style is a groundbreaking creative insight or complete nonsense. In the classroom there will be the same issues. A child cannot break the conventions of a subject area creatively and with purpose unless they understand them in the first place. For example, changing a fairy story so that we have sympathy for the giant, or so that the wolf is the misunderstood hero or the princess refuses to marry the prince, loses its impact if you do not know that this is not how conventional fairy stories usually go. You cannot make an impact by changing a rhyme scheme or the structure of a limerick unless you understand the normal conventions and have made the changes for a particular purpose. Teachers therefore need to have confidence in their own subject knowledge and yet the flexibility to recognise when and how 'rules' and conventions can be altered or ignored, and they also need to teach children the conventions within different disciplines as well as encourage them to 'play with' those conventions and see what effect that has and what they think of the results. The ideal here would be to understand the conventions but not be conventional.

 Classroom idea

PSHE, art, music etc.

Discuss and question the children's attitudes to different styles and representations, e.g. in the visual arts, music, literature, architecture, food. What do they like and why? What is being achieved and how? Does everyone like the same things? How does it make them feel? Make sure they are aware that people have very different tastes and ideas and may hold these views strongly, and that we can disagree while respecting the other person's right to hold that viewpoint.

Margaret Boden concludes, 'the "freedom" of creative thought is not the absence of constraints, but their imaginative – yet disciplined – development ... Creativity is not the same thing as knowledge, but is firmly grounded in it. What educators must try to do is to nurture the knowledge without killing the creativity' (Boden, 2001: 102).

Personal attributes and pedagogic skills

Many of the personal attributes and pedagogic skills that will enable a teacher to teach creatively and to identify, encourage and foster creativity have already been evident in this and previous chapters, but the list is long and there are more aspects to consider.

If teachers are to recognise and encourage pupil creativity they will have to be able to appreciate ideas that they might not themselves have thought of and be able to see different ways of doing things. They will need to have the empathy to recognise that what works for them might not work for others. Ken Robinson comments on an 'assumption in the Western worldview, the idea of linearity' (2001: 85). He points out that we tend to expect learning to move in a logical sequence with new learning building on previous learning 'like bricks in a wall', but that this is not always the case. Learning can sometimes be more random than that, and a 'jigsaw' approach where individual pieces come together to make a whole picture can sometimes be the way that children make sense of new and established learning. Encouraging children to use mind maps to see and plot the relationships between things and lists and timelines to examine the linearity will all be key in encouraging different kinds of thinking.

In encouraging and fostering creative responses teachers need above all to have and show respect for the individual learner. A put down, however unintentional, or ignoring an idea because it doesn't fit with your view of the progression of the lesson, may give messages to a child that you do not appreciate their contributions and they may stop contributing. Bill Lucas (2001: 40) has compiled a list of ways in which a teacher can encourage rather than stifle children's creativity:

- Being respectful rather than dismissive.
- Encouraging active not passive learning.
- Supporting individual interests rather than standardized curriculums.
- Engaging many learning styles not one.
- Encouraging and exploring emotional responses.
- Posing questions not statements.
- Offering ambiguity rather than certainties.
- Being open-ended rather than closing down.
- Being known as surprising rather than predictable.

- Offering many patterns rather than a standardized model.
- Moving the 'classroom' to varied environments.
- Recognizing multiple intelligences.
- Including visual representations as well as auditory ones.
- Including tactile and experience-based activity.
- Stimulating social as well as private learning.

Individual or group activities

1 Rank the above statements in the order you think they would impact on encouraging children's creativity. If you are working with others discuss your reasons as you do so.
2 Identify any statements you think you would find personally difficult to fulfil, that you do not agree with, or that you think might present problems in the classroom. Note down or discuss why you feel this.
3 Think of an experienced teacher whom you consider to be good at encouraging creativity in their pupils. Which of the above statements would be true of their practice?
4 Discount any statements you identified in activity 2. Of the remaining statements which do you feel are already part of your practice as a teacher? Which would you like to develop next? Set yourself a couple of individual targets to work on in the classroom.

It is important not to expect that you can do all of these things straightaway. Guy Claxton uses the phrase 'mayonnaise model' (2002: 89) as he says, 'Setting yourself clear targets, one at a time, is a very good way of blending ideas into practice and preventing them from curdling'.

A teacher who manages creative learning skilfully is going to be able to manage time successfully. The demands of the curriculum mean that there are constant decisions that have to be made as to how much time can be allocated to certain activities. To allow time for children to think and reflect and to explore, play and investigate possible avenues of enquiry and outcomes will be a constant balancing act. In 2003 an HMI report was published called *Expecting the Unexpected – Developing Creativity in Primary and Secondary Schools*. This concluded that 'Creative work also often needs unbroken time to develop. Primary schools which maintained sufficient flexibility in their timetables for lessons to be blocked or extended to accommodate planned events or just to provide more time for creative activities, found it easier to enable this kind of development' (HMI, 2003: 12). Deciding what to do if one or two children are deeply involved in a really fruitful activity while the rest of the class is ready to move on will be difficult too.

So, what can you do to make and manage the time successfully? We will look at this in more detail when we look closely at planning in Part Four, but for now think about the following:

- Not all work has to be done to the same depth. Identify which activities are the most important and allocate them more time, early on in the term. Later, if there is not time for everything you want to cover, give different activities or areas of enquiry to individual groups to work on, and then ask them to report back on their research or findings to the rest of the class.
- Work with parallel learning objectives in two or three subjects where possible. So, learning note taking can be practised with reference to research in geography, and organising the findings, drawing conclusions and writing them up can incorporate learning in both the geography and non-chronological writing. Position areas of learning that link well with others carefully on the timetable so these occur when they are most useful to you, e.g. data handling when you will need to do a survey in geography or generate data in science.
- Find a key text or texts that you can use in English which will enhance the context of the themes being studied and allow for thought and discussion in these areas.
- Block work where possible. So, for example, use three afternoons in a week for multidisciplinary work without needing to break and change from subject to subject.
- Plan time (maybe on a Friday) for extended work, applying learning from earlier in the week or pursuing long-term projects. Have shorter challenges available for those who finish before others until you need to pull findings together and move on as a class.
- Sometimes work a 'carousel' of activities so that the best use of targeted support and resources can be made.

A teacher who is successful in identifying, fostering and encouraging creativity in their pupils will be able to step back, observe and analyse the learning that is happening in the classroom. They will need to be able to reflect on what they have observed and to make decisions to balance the needs of the class, different groups and individuals. We have seen how they will need the ability to promote a culture and ethos that will support children in working creatively, and must be able to put all children at their ease but also make them feel safe by being firm, consistent and fair. Teachers are also going to have to be prepared to learn from others, including their pupils, and be good team players, relishing opportunities to team teach or work in collaboration with others. All of this means that teachers who are successful in this area will have a strong core identity, being confident in themselves so they are prepared to take risks and be flexible but also reflective and analytical in order that their decisions are taken in the best interests of the children's learning. Mathilda Marie Joubert points out that 'Experience has shown that creative teachers constantly reinvent themselves and adapt their teaching styles and strategies to different situations as required ... If teachers remain firmly rooted in terms of their identity and core principles it allows them to feel free to use flexibility in terms of what they do' (2001: 22). In the early days and years of a teaching career that core identity is still developing and so are the skills to support it, but small steps can lead to significant results even during a teacher's training, and working creatively brings benefits to the teacher as well as the children. Joubert puts it succinctly: 'This is a difficult but exciting and rewarding process, which could prevent stagnation and mental starvation' (2001: 22).

 Personal thought and reflection

Above we used the phrase 'core identity'. Imagine you are about to retire after a long and successful teaching career. A trusted colleague will make a speech about your strengths as a teacher. What would you want them to say about you? Jot down the points you would want to hear about yourself. Now think about the teacher you are at present. Obviously you lack the experience of the 'retiring' teacher, but which of the points you jotted down are developing already in your practice? Can you sum up your 'core identity' as a teacher at present in 15 words or less? Record this somewhere and date it (perhaps inside the cover of this book), and then return to this activity in the future and see how or if that 'core identity' has changed.

Chapter summary

In this chapter we have looked at the importance of recognising your own creativity and using it to model creative processes for children. We have seen how examining our own creativity can lead to us understanding better the creativity of the children we teach. We have looked at ways to identify creativity in others and how to foster and encourage creativity once this has been identified. We have also discovered many of the personal attributes necessary to be a successful creative teacher, and begun to identify the skills that need to be mastered to encourage and foster creativity in the children we teach.

Further study

Critical Reflection: Activity 5

Allow an hour for this activity.

You have just *identified* your core identity. Choose one aspect of this that you believe flourishes in your role as a primary teacher. *Synthesise* the evidence that leads you to believe this.

Choose one aspect of your core identity that is less well developed. How could you use the strength identified above to develop this aspect of yourself? *Identify* the first steps you need to take to make progress on this journey.

Now, look from the perspective of the children you are teaching. *Identify* a child whom you think is not achieving as much as they could. *Identify* one of that child's creative aspects which they seem to enjoy. *Analyse* how you think you could use this aspect more fully to enable that child to progress.

 Further reading

Craft, A., Gardner, H. and Claxton, G. (eds) (2008) *Creativity, Wisdom and Trusteeship: Exploring the Role of Education*. Thousand Oaks, CA: Corwin.

HMI (2003) *Expecting the Unexpected – Developing Creativity in Primary and Secondary Schools*. HMI 1612. London: Ofsted.

Robinson, K. (2001) *Out of Our Minds*. Oxford: Capstone.

CHAPTER 6

KEY SKILLS FOR THE CREATIVE TEACHER

 Learning objectives in this chapter:

To look in more depth at particular skills that are useful to the creative teacher, including:

- Facilitating
- Questioning
- Using a sketchbook/scrapbook approach
- Motivating
- Using drama techniques

Relevant Teachers' Standards for this chapter

A teacher must:

5   Adapt teaching to respond to the strengths and needs of all pupils

5a   know when and how to differentiate appropriately, using approaches which enable pupils to be taught effectively

(Continued)

(Continued)

5d   have a clear understanding of the needs of all pupils, including those with special educational needs; those of high ability; those with English as an additional language; those with disabilities; and be able to use and evaluate distinctive teaching approaches to engage and support them

7   **Manage behaviour effectively to ensure a good and safe learning environment**

7b   have high expectations of behaviour, and establish a framework for discipline with a range of strategies, using praise, sanctions and rewards consistently and fairly

In this chapter we are going to look more closely at some of the skills, ideas and methods that have been introduced in previous chapters. In a single chapter this will necessarily be only an introduction to what are, in some cases, complex methodologies. You are encouraged to follow up areas of interest in more depth in the texts referred to.

Every teacher develops their own style in the classroom. Whether you are naturally a quite loud and bouncy character or more quiet and reflective will transmit itself into your 'teaching persona'. However, there are certain methodologies or teaching styles that can be practised and learned. Experienced teachers often become so used to the ways they organise their class or phrase questions that they may have become unaware of the strategies they are using or unable to appreciate the skills they have learned. On being questioned on their methodology they may need time to analyse and 'unpick' their practice so they can share strategies that are successful. While strategies are new they require constant attention and practice until they become habitual. If they are replacing other, older habits they will need even more repetition until the brain has created and 'hard wired' the response as a default position. If this proves difficult, it would be good to remember that this is exactly what we are asking children to do when we want them to change their behaviour or ways of working.

 Individual or group activity

Read the following short playscript. If possible read it aloud in a group, taking parts as necessary.

After you have read this, discuss the questions that follow it before continuing to read the second playscript.

A Classroom Somewhere – 1

Paula: Alright everyone. Let's have you looking this way. Anton, can you turn round please? Thank you. Now, this afternoon we're going to look at solids and liquids. As you can see I've written the aim on the board, we're going to learn the differences between solids and liquids and their properties. What are properties? Sarah?

Sarah:	What they do.
Paula:	That's right. What they do. How we recognise them. First I've got these wooden blocks. What are they?
Anton:	Wooden blocks.
Paula:	Yes, Anton, they're wooden blocks, but are they solid or liquid? Uroosa?
Uroosa:	Solid, miss.
Paula:	Quite right. And how do we know?
Abisola:	They keep their shape.
Paula:	Good. If I tip them into this container they still stay the same shape. What happens if I tip some water from this jug into the container? First of all what do we call it if we tip liquid?
Sarah:	Pouring.
Paula:	Right. Liquids pour, solids don't. And then what happens to it in the container?
Abisola:	It takes the shape of the container.
Paula:	Good. And that's one of the properties of liquids, they take the shape of the container they're in.
Uroosa:	And they pour, miss.
Paula:	Yes, they pour.
Edward:	What about sand?
Paula:	What about sand, Edward?
Edward:	Well, sand would take the shape of the container too.
Paula:	But sand's not a liquid.
Edward:	I know, but it pours and it takes the shape of the container.
Paula:	But the little grains of sand don't change shape.
Edward:	But if it has the properties of a liquid it must be a liquid.
Paula:	But the sand itself doesn't change shape. If I add another drop of water to this water what happens? Amy?
Amy:	[shakes her head]
Paula:	Have a try, Amy.
Amy:	[mumbles] I dunno.

(Continued)

(Continued)

Paula:	Sam?
Sam:	It joins on?
Paula:	Yes, that's a good way of describing it. You can't tell which drop I just put in. And what can you tell me about the surface of the water?
Abisola:	It's always flat.
Paula:	Yes. It finds its own level and that's another property of liquids.
Edward:	But, miss...
Paula:	Yes, Edward?
Edward:	What about waves? They're not flat.
Paula:	No, Edward they're not. But that's because...

Discussion

(If you are working alone, try to note down your responses to these questions.) What is happening in this classroom? How is the teacher organising the lesson? What strategies is she using? What do you think works and what do you think is not so effective? Why?

Prompts for discussion

After some time for discussion look at the following prompts and address any points you have not already covered:

- How does the teacher introduce the lesson?
- What type/s of questioning does she use?
- How does she deal with Edward's question? Why do you think that is? What other agendas might be going on here?
- Who is the child who seems to know all the answers? Is she learning anything?
- What learning is happening in the lesson? Who for?

Now read the second playscript and discuss this in the same way.

A Classroom Somewhere – 2

(Amy's and Edward's parents have moved them to this new school so they appear again here.)

Kim:	As you can see on your tables you've got lots of equipment – containers, sieves, cloths, kitchen roll and a jug of water, some washing-up liquid, honey, blocks, plastic shapes ... We are going to be looking at solids and liquids this afternoon. What are they?

What are their properties? How can we tell the difference between them? I've written the questions up there to remind you. So, first of all in your groups have a talk and think of some more detailed questions you could ask or some lines of investigation you could follow.

Bill: How about mixing stuff together. Like you could mix the liquids together but could you mix the solids together?

Natalie: But that's boring 'cos you know the answer already.

Olu: No you don't. You could mix like salt and talcum powder together and you wouldn't know the difference.

Bill: But they wouldn't have *mixed*.

Julia: I suppose if you squashed something. Like, you know, if you liquidise a carrot and an apple then you could mix them.

Natalie: Yeah, but you're *liquidising* them. You're turning them into a liquid.

Julia: But they're still little bits of carrot and apple. They're not really a liquid. It's not like they melted.

Bill: Miss! If you liquidise a carrot is it still a solid?

Kim: I'm not sure. Does it split it into tiny solid bits in liquid? I really don't know. Why? What were you trying to find out?

Olu: Whether only liquids will mix together.

Natalie: Or can you make some solids mix together.

Julia: And will all liquids mix? 'Cos I've just thought of some that don't.

Kim: Well why don't you start with the mixing test for things you *know* are solids or liquids. But hang on to the idea about liquidising food. Is there a way to find out if it's really turned into a liquid? That really addresses the question 'what is a liquid?'. Put it on a sticky note. We need to come back to that.

(Meanwhile …)

Edward: I tell you something that's always worried me.

Keisha: What?

Edward: Sand. They say liquids pour but sand pours too. And liquids take the shape of the container they're in but sand does too. So why is sand not a liquid?

Keisha: It won't always pour. Sand on the beach doesn't pour.

(Continued)

(Continued)

Amy:	That's because it's wet.
Keisha:	Yeah, but when it's wet you can build with it. Sandcastles. You couldn't build with a liquid.
Amy:	But you've changed it by wetting it. You could change water by freezing it into ice and making shapes. That's not fair.
Grant:	But even dry sand will make a pile. It doesn't go flat like water.
Kelly:	Soaking.
Grant:	What?
Kelly:	Soaking. A liquid would soak through into kitchen towel or tissue. Sand would lie on top. So it's a solid.
Grant:	Yeah. Like filtering. Only liquids go through.
Edward:	Do they?
Keisha:	Well let's try it. We say liquids will go through filter paper and solids won't. That's the difference.
Kim:	This sounds like a good idea. Give it a try. Plan it out and find a way to record it. And you might like to check out Toronto group's sticky note. I think you might be able to solve their problem.

Discussion

(If you are working alone, try to note down your responses to these questions.) What is happening in this classroom? How is the teacher organising the lesson? What strategies is she using? What are the differences from the first classroom?

Prompts for discussion

After some time for discussion, look at the following prompts and address any points you have not already covered:

- How does the teacher introduce the lesson?
- How does the teacher organise the lesson?
- What learning is happening in the lesson? Who for?
- Were the children being creative? If so, in what ways? What potential for more creative learning was there?

Issues

- Teacher Paula is very clear about the points she wants to cover but her questioning is quite closed and she has expectations about the 'right' answers she expects. She tries to answer Edward's question but it feels as if she is out of her depth and wants to steer the lesson back to where she is comfortable. All questioning and responses happen between teacher and pupil, there is no discussion.

- Teacher Kim introduces her learning intentions as learning questions to investigate. She is happy to say that she does not know an answer to a question (this may be true or she may be dissembling – not knowing can sometimes be a good strategy to stimulate enquiry). She facilitates the children's discussion and enquiry.
- Teacher Paula is demonstrating with practical equipment but the children are not handling it themselves. Teacher Kim has equipment available and the children will investigate their ideas in a hands-on way.
- In the second classroom the children have very good discussion and group skills. They are happy to take other people's ideas and move them on, to disagree without falling out and to use prior learning experience from their lives both inside and outside school. These skills do not develop overnight; the children have obviously been used to working in groups like this for some time.
- Teacher Kim facilitates the groups' working: she steers one group (who may be less able) to concentrate on investigating things they know are solids and liquids, and passes the question of 'liquefying' solids on to another group who are more able to investigate it.
- Edward is able to discuss his queries in the second classroom and have them dealt with. Even Amy feels able to contribute ideas.

Facilitating

When children are working in groups, there may often be times when the teacher takes on the role of facilitator, as in the second scene above. In this role the teacher works with individuals and groups to help them take responsibility for their own learning. There has been much research and writing about facilitating groups in work and business situations as well as in education (see for example Belbin, 1981; Schwartz, 2002). This tends to break down into two types of groups: those that are charged with finding solutions to a problem, and those that are more therapeutic and involved with exploring and changing attitudes and behaviours.

From both processes there are some guidelines as to how a facilitator can function most effectively and how the role differs from the more didactic roles of a teacher. The sections in earlier chapters on group work and creating a supportive environment are essential prerequisites of a good facilitator. Other things to consider are:

- The facilitator does not take on a decision making function but is there to increase the group's effectiveness. They are not a leader in this situation.
- Facilitators will need to intervene, make suggestions and offer insights. They might ask questions, summarise what has been said thus far or make observations or comments, but overall they will say relatively little.
- The facilitator needs to show that individual participants and their contributions are valued and understood.

- Group members need to be clear about what the session's purpose is. The facilitator may need to intervene as necessary to clarify the goal and help the group achieve it.
- Timings most usefully take the first quarter to establish the issue that needs exploring, the middle half in engaging with the subject and developing understanding, and the final quarter in taking stock, identifying goals and planning subsequent actions and development.
- A facilitator might have to identify and highlight any problems that are holding the group back. This may mean challenging any inappropriate behaviour.
- Thought has to be given to the composition of the group and recognising the various roles that operate within it. Belbin (1981) identified various roles that were needed in groups both for making the task prosper and the group function well; he also identified the roles that may sabotage the smooth working of a group. If you have two people who are in conflict it may be that they both normally operate in the same role, for example as an initiator or opinion giver. A group that is going round in circles may have no one giving it direction or summarising. Making sure groups are well balanced takes time and knowledge of the children involved.

Questioning

Guy Claxton makes the point, 'Good learners like questions, and are not afraid of the "don't know" state of mind out of which questions emerge' (2002: 25). In the second playscript above both the children and the teacher were asking questions as a route to their investigation of solids and liquids. In the first playscript only the teacher was posing questions, to which she already knew the answers. (Apart from Edward, who did not get much further forward with his question.)

Claxton demonstrates how questioning is not just the ability to ask good questions but also 'the disposition to do so (which is sometimes called curiosity)'. He also points out the often-missed idea that questioning can be non-verbal just as much as verbal. The process of 'playing around' with materials or ideas which is such a strong element of creativity is in itself a form of questioning.

So, in a creative classroom, the teacher will need to have good questioning skills but will also have to establish a questioning and enquiring culture in that classroom.

In Oxford Brookes University's useful briefing document on questioning (unfortunately no longer available) these characteristics of a genuine climate of enquiry are given:

- Questions being used only to demonstrate real and not pretended curiosity (especially by the teacher).
- Active, responsive listening, e.g. a willingness to let talk change one's view.

- The allowance of quality thinking time, including 'comfortable' silences.
- Signs of thoughtfulness when speaking, e.g. searching for the best wording, or giving answers in the form of further questions.
- The use of questioning as part of an ongoing dialogue, and not to start and stop dialogue.
- A lack of fear of raising puzzling questions (on the part of teacher and pupils).

The most influential writing on questioning in education remains that based on Bloom's Taxonomy. Published in 1956, Bloom and other educational researchers classified statements of educational objectives in the cognitive domain in a hierarchy from less to more complex (Bloom et al., 1956). These were originally ordered as Knowledge, Comprehension, Application, Analysis, Synthesis and Evaluation. There has been some debate as to whether the last two levels should be reversed. Many educationalists have produced helpful guides to using questions to stimulate learning in the different areas. Research has shown that teachers tend to ask questions in the 'Knowledge' category to check recall or understanding of facts 80% to 90% of the time (Wragg and Brown, 2001), and only to encourage pupils to think around 10% of the time.

For a useful chart that can be used to plan questions and activities that will stimulate learning in these 'higher order' domains consult *Extending Children's Special Abilities – Strategies in the Primary Classroom* (Dalton and Smith, 1986; Curriculum Branch, Schools Division), which can be found on several websites.

 Classroom idea

Thinking skills

This activity, although apparently simple, can help stimulate higher order thinking skills.

Children can work alone or in pairs. Each child or pair is given a digital camera (or they can use a mobile phone camera if allowed) and a small card frame. The frame should be about A5 size. Each frame has a word written on it.

Useful words to use are:

Table 6.1

dangerous	peaceful	disappointing	worrying	fun
yellow	intricate	inspiring	light	soft
curious	intriguing	exciting	complicated	green
complex	powerful	exuberant		

(Continued)

(Continued)

Children are asked to use a specific space (school grounds and classroom, local park) and then use the frame to frame a particular object or view that represents their word and to photograph it. They should find and photograph five different images each exemplifying their word. They then share and explain their selection.

This is a fun, hands-on activity, but having to find five examples challenges interpretations of the word and its implications. Children have to select, analyse, apply, and evaluate and justify their choices.

(Passed on by Jonathan Barnes and Stephen Scoffham.)

 Individual activity

Observe a lesson or use a video of a lesson. Which types of questioning are being used? What is the balance of questions posed by the teacher and by the children? Which levels of Bloom's Taxonomy are being addressed?

Plan an activity that will encourage children to use the four higher levels of Bloom's Taxonomy in their thinking (application, analysis, synthesis and evaluation).

A useful website for more guidance on good questioning is found at www.fromgoodtooutstanding.com/2012/05/ofsted-2012-questioning-to-promote-learning.

The sketchbook/scrapbook approach

In previous chapters we looked briefly at the possibilities of keeping various sorts of notebooks. If these are to be useful then children will need to spend some time learning how to use them constructively and creatively, and the teacher will have to remind the children of their use and application frequently until their use becomes second nature.

Many schools use sketchbooks in art for the children to record particular details of texture or tone, of colour, a particular view or unusual angle. These may be sketches but might also be cuttings from magazines, found objects, postcards or photographs. Children are then encouraged to use what they have 'collected' in their sketchbook to inform their composition in a particular art form.

The same method can be used to collect, sample, observe and record in a number of different areas. Words or phrases that excite or intrigue can be jotted down, ideas for titles, random 'what if' thoughts or descriptions of people observed or invented could all form part of an author's journal to be used when composing narrative or poetry. Questions, observations, hypotheses or ideas to try could be part of a scientific notebook. These could reflect interesting results when investigations did not turn out as expected or the random thoughts that sometimes occur in everyday situations. (Why is the pigeon pecking at that leaf? I didn't think they ate leaves. Why do my glasses steam up when I walk into a warm room?) An inventor's notebook could include ideas for tools or objects when a need is identified (adjustable legs on school tables and chairs so that different heights can be accommodated), observations of joints and movements, questions and notes about materials.

Just recording these ideas and questions will mean very little if the children are not given time to consider and explore them. Try choosing a time about once a half-term when the class will look through their notebooks and choose something they want to use or investigate further. Discussing their choices (or even going through their notebooks) with a partner can help in justifying these and planning out possible lines of action. A day could be set aside when the planned activities generated from this session could be undertaken. This could be either singly or groups or pairs could agree to collaborate on one child's ideas or combine their efforts if they were compatible (further ideas for making and using sketchbooks are to be found at www.accessart.org.uk/sketchbook).

Motivation

Being able to motivate children to learn well is one of the most useful skills a teacher can have. When a child is motivated to learn their own impetus takes over and the teacher is able to guide, provide a structure and information, suggest methods of working and pose questions, and the child will willingly take them forward.

Motivation is often classified in two ways: *extrinsic*, when we are motivated by the possible results of what we do (from winning a prize or getting a good mark to winning praise or, conversely, fear of punishment), and *intrinsic*, when we are motivated by the experience itself and find it rewarding in its own right. A third type of motivation is sometimes added here, i.e. *internal* motivation, when a task is not intrinsically motivating but the person recognises that it will be worth doing in the long run. This obviously requires a recognition of the importance of delayed gratification. (For more examination of motivation and how it relates to different learning theories, the chapter 'Looking at learning' by David Wray in Arthur and Cremin's (2010) book might be useful.)

Teachers tend to use a lot of extrinsic motivation. They offer stickers or merit points, smiles and praise, and there is the threat of sanctions or the withdrawing of those smiles and praise if the wrong behaviour is exhibited. However, if only extrinsic motivation is used a child does not necessarily learn to motivate themself or to understand the importance of the task for its own sake. It can also result in the teacher's role being more that of a 'puppet master'. How many teachers have despaired when they return to their classroom after a supply teacher has been with their class and find the pencils broken and thrown around? 'But you know how to behave, you know these things belong to you, and if you don't look after them you won't have them to use,' the teacher says, but the internal motivation to look after their equipment wasn't strong enough. In both learning and behaviour trying to make a transition between extrinsic motivation to internal and, hopefully, intrinsic motivation will be important. In motivating children to learn well there are a number of things that teachers can do.

 Personal thought and reflection

The following activity comes from the SEAL staff materials (DfES, 2005).

There are some teaching strategies that are thought to encourage internal motivation in learners. Some of these are included in the table below. Rate yourself according to how frequently you use the strategies in the table.

Table 6.2

Strategy	Seldom									Often
• Show a personal enjoyment, interest and enjoyment in the content of the lesson	1	2	3	4	5	6	7	8	9	10
• Place an emphasis on how children learn rather than their performance	1	2	3	4	5	6	7	8	9	10
• Encourage autonomy in children	1	2	3	4	5	6	7	8	9	10
• Focus on individual improvement and what has been learned rather than making judgements or comparisons	1	2	3	4	5	6	7	8	9	10
• Emphasise progress over time rather than grades or marks	1	2	3	4	5	6	7	8	9	10
• Provide informative feedback that helps the child feel responsible for their success and helps them improve	1	2	3	4	5	6	7	8	9	10
• Attribute failure to the nature of the task, quality of teaching or some changeable aspect of the child	1	2	3	4	5	6	7	8	9	10
• Make it clear that mistakes are a valuable part of learning	1	2	3	4	5	6	7	8	9	10

Think of examples in your own or other teachers' practice that demonstrate these attributes. Which do you think are the most difficult to achieve?

Observing what children find intrinsically motivating can be very useful. If a majority of the class love team games or singing or drama then using those as techniques to teach other subjects can be very motivating. For example, there are lots of ways to learn and practise number bonds and operations by inventing team games so you could try a game where the children run up and put two numbered beanbags in a bucket marked with the appropriate operation to make a required total.

Putting learning in an authentic or realistic situation can also really motivate children to learn. An authentic situation is one where the activity reflects life outside the classroom (see Craft, 2005: 60). There are often possibilities for writing in different genres; older children could visit children in younger classes (many schools make time for paired reading partners between different classes) and discover what type of stories the children like, how they are constructed (e.g. the use of rhyme or repetition), the type of characters they like. These can then be adopted by the older children to write and illustrate a story for their reading partner; they can then also develop and use their craft skills to make a durable book, perhaps with pop-ups or flaps if appropriate. An investigation in geography that identifies a need for improving the local area could lead to letters to the local council, allowing children to use their skills in persuasive formal letter writing.

 Classroom example

Cross-curricular

In a school that used certificates and stickers for reward and motivation, a class researched which types were most often used and any that teachers would like which did not at present exist. They asked children which images and wording inspired them. The class then designed a range of their own certificates and stickers using different art media and digital media. They investigated the prices for card, printable labels, colour photocopies and printing, and worked out if they could manufacture and distribute their own range to the school more cheaply than those bought from a catalogue. They then produced and marketed their range within the school and saw the results used in celebration assemblies and classrooms for the rest of the year.

As well as exploiting opportunities that occur naturally in the school, teachers can think ahead to plan for opportunities for learning to happen in authentic situations. The example of writing story books for a younger audience, used above, would obviously involve forward planning and cooperation between the class teachers. Some situations for learning can be 'simulated' by using low-key role-play techniques. For instance, the example of the children writing letters to the council about their geography work could be extended and enhanced by this method. The unit of work could be initiated by a letter, supposedly from the local council, asking the children to submit plans for redeveloping a particular building or piece of land in the locality. The children would have to plan their strategies, conduct surveys among local residents and workers about needs and opinions, formulate ideas, use maps and plans, calculate areas, use percentages, handle data, design solutions, and prepare written submissions and presentations to put forward their ideas. This would be a significant unit of work covering several subject areas, probably spread over half a term. By putting the 'need' to learn and display certain skills within a context that the children feel to be authentic, even though recognising that it is simulated, they engage in that learning with a will. They can see the purpose of what they are doing and the fact that they are doing it for an outside agency will motivate them to 'up their game' and do the very best they can. More complex examples of working in this way and advice as to how to plan in this way will appear in later chapters.

Using drama techniques

The last example used low-level role-play techniques to put learning in a more authentic context and enhance motivation. Drama and role-play can play a significant part in allowing children to learn in creative ways. Drama techniques need to be practised and developed in the same way as any other skills. Children cannot be expected to be able to use a particular technique without explanation and practice. Even a seemingly simple technique such as hotseating will be of little value unless the children understand how it can be used and have sufficient time to learn how to do it well and prepare for it. However, taking the time to develop drama skills is time well spent as these can enhance learning in many ways. Some of the benefits from using drama are:

- children can engage emotionally with the subject matter;
- it encourages learning in practical, physical ways;
- it can allow children who have difficulty with reading and writing to learn and demonstrate what they have learned in a different way;
- children can 'rehearse' different opinions, reactions or ways of interacting with others in a secure environment;
- learning can be more memorable;
- it can build self-confidence and presentation skills.

Learning to use drama techniques is a long and complex process and would take far more space and time than are possible within this chapter, but some entry points follow below, one more fully worked, and there are examples of lesson plans and planning using drama in the chapters on planning which follow. For further reading, Patrice Baldwin's *The Primary Drama Handbook: An Introduction* (Baldwin, 2008) or Mike Fleming's *Starting Drama Teaching* (Fleming, 2011) are useful starting points.

Classroom example

Drama, History

The example uses drama to teach about Stone Age Britain by utilising the 'teacher talk-through with occupational mime' technique.

Explain to the children that they should listen very carefully to your voice as you narrate what is happening. They don't have to work in silence but should always be able to hear your voice. They should follow what you are narrating and act it out.

Ask the children to lie down on the floor and close their eyes. As you narrate the story, take part as well, miming the activities and adding dialogue. Begin the narration.

You are still asleep but the sky is just beginning to get lighter. Morning is on its way. You begin to stir and stretch. You sit up, it's still quite cold so you wrap yourself in your cloak, it's newly woven and warm. There is some cold meat still left on the bones from last night and a hunk of bread so you eat that to break your fast. You tie on your shoes, pick up the stone axe you know you will need, tie your pouch to your belt and move to the door of your house, untie the leather hanging over the doorway and come outside.

Today you are going to work together to finish the new house you are building. Your homes have got very crowded as your village grows in size so the new house will be very welcome. You know you will need more hazel branches to finish the walls and roof of the house so you walk away from your houses to the stand of trees where the hazel trees grow. You choose thin branches to weave in and out of the thick posts you have already fixed into the earth. Taking your axe you cut down the branches you need. It's hard work and you're soon sweating. You notice that the stone axehead is getting loose in its handle – you must tie it in more securely later. You gather up the branches and carry them back to the half-finished house. You stand around the circular house and weave the hazel branches in and out of the posts.

When you've finished you go to the place where you left the chalk you cut from the hillside with antler picks. Place it on a big skin. It needs to be crushed up into powder with big hard stones. Bash it and crush it until it's all powdered. Now fetch the straw you've been keeping for this and mix it with the chalk. You need some water. Get the leather bucket and go down to the stream and scoop up some water. Come back to the chalk mix and add the water and squidge it up into a thick paste. Carry the skin with the chalk paste on it over to the house. It will take several of you to carry. Some work inside the house and some outside and press the chalk plaster through the woven hazel to fill up all the gaps. Don't leave any gaps or the wind and rain will get in.

(Continued)

(Continued)

Continue the narration to thatch the roof and fix a newly-cured skin over the doorway. Perhaps end by bringing stones for the hearth in the centre of the new house and lighting a fire using flint and iron pyrite (kept carefully in their pouches).

Signal to the children that the drama has finished by changing the pitch and tone of your voice out of narrator and back to teacher. Ask the children what they know about the people they were pretending to be. Encourage speculation with further questions. What tools did they use? What were they made of? What shape were their houses? What were their clothes made of? Establish that they lived as a community, they worked hard and worked together, they were a settled community. Their tools were made from different kinds of stone. They knew how to weave (and probably kept sheep to use the wool to spin and weave) and cured animal hides for leather. They used cereal crops (bread and straw). And so on. Point out to the children how much they already know about these people. When do they think they lived? (Roughly the new Stone Age [Neolithic] as they lived in a permanent community and farmed crops and animals.)

This technique is a wonderful, practical way of communicating information without just talking at the children. Their physical participation makes it more likely they will identify with the period, build empathy for the people, and understand how they lived.

Follow-up activity

How would you continue this introduction to Stone Age life? How often and to what extent could you continue to use this drama technique in subsequent sessions? How would you balance it with research in the classroom or practical activities like spinning with a drop spindle or weaving? How could this take you into written work?

Think about the drama activity and which other subjects or history study units it could be useful for.

How might you incorporate outdoor learning in this study unit?

 ## Classroom ideas

Drama

'We have received a letter/email asking for our help.'

Like the local area planning example above, this activity can provide a motivation for learning in different areas. In this example a single message may set out the whole activity. However, a series of communications may stimulate different activities or phases of the activity. In the 'Quest' example in Chapter 9, a series of letters from a mythical figure prompts the children to go on a quest that involves learning in several different subject areas. The 'drama' may consist of quite short 'pretend' sessions of miming packing bags, travelling in different ways etc. The teacher acts as facilitator, remaining in role as teacher but maintaining the fiction: 'Well, if we are going to help Salazar what do we need to do first?'

'I need volunteers/workers to help me.'

In this scenario the teacher is in role. They might be a sea captain seeking recruits to sail on a voyage of discovery, a factory owner needing employees, a Victorian housekeeper training new servants in a big house. The first sessions will involve training the new recruits using occupational mime and interactions that set the scene: 'Now, you must always be very quiet when you're in the part of the house where the family live. They don't want to see servants with dirty coal scuttles. So, pick up your bucket very quietly – it's heavy I know, but you'll soon get used to it.' This can be a good introduction to using role-play areas, giving verbal and movement vocabulary to the children for them to reuse themselves later. It can also lead to an episodic drama so in each session the new sailors meet a different situation, from a storm at sea to staking claim to a 'new' territory, where the drama provides a stimulus to further research, debate or writing.

'I'm going to tell a story and I want you to help me.'

This technique is more fully described in Chapter 9 as the 'Shoe Shop' lesson. It involves the teacher as narrator 'telling' a story that asks the children to join in as different characters and undertake different roles within it. For example: 'Molly walked down the road. Would you like to be Molly? As she approached the market she saw two of the stallholders arguing about where their stalls should be. Will you two be the stall holders? Let's hear what you're saying.' This can either be geared to focus on the activities that are undertaken (as in the Shoe Shop example) or to focus on situations that might need sorting out (how could the argument be resolved?).

Forum theatre

This can be an ideal way of looking at issues in PSHE. The children sit round in a circle and volunteers start acting out a situation: for example, a child asking their parent for something they really want. If the 'audience' sees anything they think the child character is doing wrong or could do better they can call out 'Stop'. The action stops and the child is invited to give advice to the character as to how they could behave differently or what they could say more effectively. An audience member could also be invited to swap with the character and step into the action to show how it could go.

(Continued)

(Continued)

Act it out

Many scientific or physical processes can be more easily understood by acting them out in mime or movement. If learning about the circulation of the blood, try establishing four children as the heart. They stand in pairs with arms raised and linked like arches, stepping forward and back to form the 'beat'. Other children are the lungs to either side, the head, legs and arms. The rest of the children are red blood cells. One after the other they enter the heart, exit to the lungs to pick up oxygen, re-enter the next chamber of the heart, and are then pushed out to take the oxygen to whichever part of the body needs it. (The brain, arms, legs etc. are calling out for oxygen as they are working.)

Chapter summary

This chapter has taken a closer look at some of the key skills for a creative teacher. These included facilitating, questioning, using a sketchbook/scrapbook approach, motivating and using drama techniques.

 Personal thought and reflection

Think back to the playscripts at the beginning of this chapter. Which of the skills outlined in this chapter were in operation there? If you were asked to teach that topic how could you incorporate other aspects that have been described? Choose another lesson or sequence of lessons that you have taught or seen taught; which of these skills were in evidence? How could you incorporate some, or all, of the techniques discussed in this chapter? Which would you choose and why?

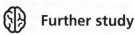 **Further study**
Critical reflection: Activity 6

Allow an hour for this activity.

In this chapter, five areas were identified for discussion: facilitating, questioning, sketchbook/scrapbook approach, motivation and drama techniques. From these five, choose one that you would like to use more effectively. *Identify* the skills you already possess in this area. *Synthesise* the evidence that leads you to believe this.

Evaluate your current work in this area by considering your strengths, limitations, what you have tried, how effective what you have tried has proved to be, what your anxieties or concerns in this area are, and what might hinder your progress.

Identify the first steps you want to take to improve in this area. Make a plan for how you are going to take these steps. What will you plan? How much time will it need? How will you make it manageable?

Identify what effect you want these changes to have on children's learning. How are you going to monitor and evaluate those changes? Make a firm plan of what you are going to do to activate this change and how you are going to *evaluate* its effects.

 Further reading

Belbin, R.M. (2010) *Management Teams: Why They Succeed or Fail*, 3rd edn. Oxford: Elsevier.

Bloom, B., Englehart, M., Furst, E., Hill, W. and Krathwohl, D. (1956) *Taxonomy of Educational Objectives: The Classification of Educational Goals. Handbook 1: Cognitive Domain*. New York: David McKay.

Fleming, M. (2011) *Starting Drama Teaching*, 3rd edn. London: David Fulton.

PART 4

A CREATIVE CURRICULUM

This final part of the book aims to help you put all you have learned into practice. It examines how to plan for creative outcomes, how to assess creatively and to assess creativity, and how to plan in cross-curricular ways, including how to plan with parallel learning objectives, knowing when to make links and when to teach subjects discretely. In order to do this it examines and comments on case studies from a variety of primary classrooms. This begins with looking at how key elements of creativity can be used in planning individual lessons. It also shows how creative elements can be added to a more standard lesson and highlights additional considerations from research. From here we consider how to plan for creative outcomes in medium-term planning or a sequence of lessons. Useful planning checklists are provided to guide and inform the planning process, and the thought processes and considerations for you as a teacher are exemplified in the case studies and commentaries.

CHAPTER 7

PLANNING FOR AND ASSESSING CREATIVE OUTCOMES

 Learning objectives in this chapter:

- To review the characteristics of creativity in teaching and learning with a view to using these to plan for creative outcomes
- To consider how to select relevant characteristics and incorporate these in lesson planning
- To consider how to keep a balance between developing skills in working creatively and opportunities to practise those skills in creative contexts
- To find the creative possibilities in each National Curriculum subject
- To consider how assessment can be undertaken in creative ways

Relevant Teachers' Standards for this chapter

A teacher must:

1   **Set high expectations which inspire, motivate and challenge pupils**

1b   Set goals that stretch and challenge pupils of all backgrounds, abilities and dispositions

(Continued)

(Continued)

2   **Promote good progress and outcomes by pupils**

2b   be aware of pupils' capabilities and their prior knowledge, and plan teaching to build on these

4   **Plan and teach well structured lessons**

4d   reflect systematically on the effectiveness of lessons and approaches to teaching

6   **Make accurate and productive use of assessment**

6a   know and understand how to assess the relevant subject and curriculum areas, including statutory assessment requirements

6b   make use of formative and summative assessment to secure pupils' progress

6d   give pupils regular feedback, both orally and through accurate marking, and encourage pupils to respond to the feedback

Now that we have looked in some detail at what creative teaching and learning might involve and what this might look like, it is time to consider how to plan lessons and activities that will foster and encourage learning in these areas.

To begin with, let us look at a lesson planned without aspirations to be creative in any particular way and see how it could be adapted to encourage more creative thinking and creative outcomes for the children and how it could be set in a more creative learning context to encourage greater motivation and engagement.

 Classroom example

Maths

Original maths lesson

The lesson is a maths lesson for 6 year olds (Year 1) with these learning objectives:

- Solve problems involving counting, adding or subtracting in the context of number.
- Relate addition to counting on and recognise that addition can be done in any order. Use practical and informal written methods to support the addition of a one-digit number or a multiple of 10 to a one-digit or two-digit number.
- Understand subtraction as 'take away' and find a 'difference' by counting up. Use practical and informal written methods to support the subtraction of a one-digit number from a one-digit or two-digit number and a multiple of 10 from a two-digit number.
- Use the vocabulary related to addition and subtraction and symbols to describe and record addition and subtraction number sentences.

The teacher planned to 'warm up' in the mental oral starter by using the interactive whiteboard (IWB) to generate addition 'questions' such as 'four flowers and five more flowers – how many all together?' which the children would answer using their number fans. The number sentence would be written on the board in each case. She would then demonstrate subtraction by 'taking away' using similar graphics on the IWB and again writing the number sentence. The children would then complete a worksheet, filling in the answers to addition and subtraction calculations, using blocks to support their calculation before recording the answers.

Now this is a perfectly adequate plan for a perfectly adequate lesson but there are certainly ways that it could be made more motivating and engaging. It could draw on and make connections with ideas from other subject areas and allow the children more autonomy in making decisions and investigating outcomes.

So, first, it could be put in a more 'authentic' context. A popular text used in Year 1 classrooms is *Handa's Surprise* by Eileen Browne (Walker Books, 1993). If the class didn't already know the text it could have been introduced in a previous Literacy lesson. (It will soon become obvious that a creative approach to planning and teaching almost always involves going beyond a single lesson. For the purposes of clarity and simplicity this example is being kept as far as possible to a single lesson, but you will see how the approach actually asks for many more links and possible spin-offs.)

Within the context of *Handa's Surprise*, the first part of the lesson could go like this:

 Classroom idea

Maths

Adapted maths lesson

Setting the scene: Remind children of the story *Handa's Surprise* by Eileen Browne.

The Activity: Gather the children on the carpet area. Ask seven children to choose a fruit (real or model) to put in Handa's basket. Count how many pieces of fruit she is starting her journey with. Choose a child to carry the basket and another to be the monkey. Make a 'pathway' through the children for Handa to walk down. When the monkey has taken one of the fruits, model writing that number sentence on the board. Ask another child to be the ostrich – children in pairs then use mini-whiteboards to write the number sentence. Show and discuss. Continue acting out the story and writing each number sentence until all the fruit is gone. Repeat the

(Continued)

(Continued)

activity with seven more children, this time choosing a small number of fruits each to put in the basket. This time the animals can be more greedy and take more than one fruit. Each time the number sentence is written on the mini-whiteboards and discussed. When all the fruit is gone one child as the billy goat can tip a whole lot of tangerines into the basket. Ask the children to estimate how many are in there. Count them out together into sets of ten and however many are over. Count the sets of ten out aloud and the units. Record the total.

Instead of a ready-made worksheet, the next part of the lesson could allow the children more autonomy in generating their own calculations.

 Classroom idea

Maths

Adapted maths lesson continued

Send the children to areas of the classroom with groups of small objects to represent fruit and a container. (This could be their tables if you want to keep the activity 'contained' but open areas if they can 'act out' the interactions sensibly.) Children choose a number of fruit to start with in their 'basket' and decide how many each animal takes and record this as a number sentence. (Children could have number cards or dice to give them the numbers to use if appropriate.)

Differentiation: Lower ability children to choose/use lower numbers. Higher ability children to move on to greedy animals that take double the number card/dice roll.

In a plenary session you could share what the higher ability children have done with doubling with the intention of moving the whole class on to working with doubling next.

If we consider the changes we have made to this lesson so far, we can see that we have:

- put the learning within a more authentic context – not a real-life context to be sure, but one the children can relate to through the story;
- made links and connections between maths and literacy; they will have understood the story better by acting it out and the maths better by seeing it in a practical context they can relate to;
- provided more motivation by enabling a practical context for the learning;
- used a simple drama technique in 'acting out' the story;
- provided opportunities for working in a group.

So, we have put the learning in a more creative context, and we have taught more creatively, but what we have not done is address actual creative learning. In Chapter 1 we identified the key elements of creativity as:

- generating new ideas;
- applying known skills and ideas in different contexts;
- taking other people's ideas or starting points and moving them on or personalising them;
- communicating ideas in interesting or varied ways;
- putting different or disparate ideas together to make something new;
- working towards a goal or set of goals;
- evaluating their own or others' work;
- adapting and improving on their work in light of their own or others' evaluations.

It is worthwhile, therefore, looking at these to see if we can spot any opportunities to include any of them.

 Individual activity

Consider the lesson as it now stands and the key elements of creativity above. Can you see any possibilities for incorporating any of the creative elements in the lesson? If so, what and how?

It is important to recognise that in many situations the answer here may well be 'No'. And rightly so. We have already seen that children need to develop the skills to be creative with. This lesson is teaching and practising a key skill and concepts that the children will use for their whole lives; we do not want to confuse or complicate matters. However, once grasped, there will be opportunities for this activity to lead to other creative outcomes.

To begin with we would want to look for opportunities for the children to be creative thinkers within the subject area being taught. In the plenary it would be possible to look at the collection of number sentences that told one of the stories and ask, 'What do you notice?' Normally when teachers ask this sort of question they have some agenda as to what they want the children to pick up on, but it is perfectly possible to ask the question in an entirely open way and see what they come up with. They may, for example, be able to generalise that each time the 'plus' sign was used in a number sentence the result got bigger and with a 'minus' sign it was always smaller. This would give you useful assessment information on the child who came up with this and possibilities for asking if they knew other ways of making results with larger or smaller numbers. There are any number of alternative observations they may come up with that we can't predict. They may notice odd or even numbers, the number of their house or age.

Something may arise that is worth pursuing at that moment or in the future, but even if it doesn't you have encouraged them to look for connections or patterns. As children get older, this approach will generate many useful routes to other possible investigations. You might also ask how Handa would notice that the animals are taking her fruit. This could prompt the children to the idea of the basket getting lighter as fruit is taken and heavier as it is added, as well as investigations in weighing the contents and hypothesising on how much the weight would change on each interaction. This might link with another lovely book, *Mrs Honey's Hat* by Pam Adams (Child's Play, 1993). Here different creatures remove and add items to the hat so that it ends up completely changed. Children could make their own hat and add and subtract items, writing the number sentences and weighing the hat and individual items and hypothesising as to whether the hat will end up lighter or heavier than it started.

The activity may also generate creative learning in other curriculum areas. An open-ended creative possibility might be to ask the children how they thought Handa could take her fruit safely to the next village without the animals getting it. This would certainly generate new ideas or allow the children to use and extend ideas. These might include using products like containers with lids or things to scare the animals away, or in processes like things Handa could do to distract or drive away the animals or take a different route. Once all the children had generated their own ideas and these had been discussed, a few of the ideas could be selected for development.

This would fulfil one of the criteria for creative learning that has been identified as most successful (HMI, 2003: 9), that of providing challenges for children where there are no clear-cut solutions.

There are also possibilities for cross-curricular work in many other areas such as:

- art – animal masks, prints, basket weaving;
- science – habitats;
- D&T – healthy eating;
- PSHE – sharing;
- English – acting out a story, retelling, writing a sequential story;
- geography – mapping the story;
- dance/drama – animal movements.

 Individual or group activity

Looking at the above cross-curricular suggestions and using your knowledge of the key elements of creativity, plan an activity that would encourage creative teaching and learning and identify the features you are addressing.

Share and discuss this if working in a group.

In this lesson the learning objectives were all in maths and there were four objectives, which is quite enough without adding any more. It is, however, often possible to have parallel learning objectives in different subjects. This might still imply a dominant subject focus for the lesson but adding a learning objective in another area (for example, including an additional learning objective to do with working well in a group in a lesson on science involving an investigation). In this case some of the preparatory time at the beginning of the lesson would be spent in discussing what makes good group work and setting up expectations and challenges for the children in the way they will cooperate. At the end of the session these will be examined and outcomes discussed. How did it go? What did they manage well? What was more difficult? What could make it better in future? This would sit equally alongside the science work.

You could, however, plan a lesson that actually has as its focus two (or more) subjects together. In this case it is important to be very clear about what the children are going to be learning in these subjects. For example, in using historical fiction in an English lesson, there is a world of difference between an activity that actually addresses learning in both history and English and one that develops learning in English in a historical context or vice versa. Each of these are perfectly valid, but it is important to understand where the learning is actually planned to take place, particularly in the early days of teaching. That is not to say that real learning may not also have taken place beyond your stated intentions. When you evaluate the lesson it will be interesting to look at what other learning may have occurred but keep the planning simple and clear to begin with.

Finding the creative possibilities in each National Curriculum subject

The introductory statements of five of the eleven subjects of the National Curriculum mention creativity specifically (mathematics, art and design, computing, design & technology, and music). Others mention what we have identified as key elements of creativity, such as 'Teaching should equip pupils to ask perceptive questions, think critically, weigh evidence, sift arguments, and develop perspective and judgement' (History), and 'These types of scientific enquiry should include: observing over time; pattern seeking; identifying, classifying and grouping' (Science) (DfE, 2014).

It is possible to find and promote elements of creativity in all of the National Curriculum subjects and, of course, these can all be taught creatively. The two key elements to do with evaluation (evaluating their own or others' work and adapting and improving on their work in the light of their own or others' evaluations) can and should, of course, be applied to all subjects throughout all aspects of the work.

Below is an outline of where creative elements may be found in individual subjects. As you begin to look at subjects for their creative possibilities you will undoubtedly find many more.

English

- Thinking up a plot for a story, using imagery, creating characters. (Generating new ideas.)
- Examining and practising the techniques of authors, playwrights and poets before using and perhaps adapting these in creating a new work. (Taking other people's ideas or starting points and moving them on or personalising them.)
- Asking children to illustrate either a passage of fiction or non-fiction including as much information as they can from the passage in their picture; this shows you clearly what they have understood. (Communicating ideas in interesting or varied ways.)
- Writing a class newspaper or stories for younger pupils, rehearsing and performing a play or performance poetry. (Working towards a goal or set of goals.)
- The advice about teaching spelling, grammar and punctuation is specific that 'This is not intended to constrain or restrict teachers' creativity, but simply to provide the structure on which they can construct exciting lessons' (DfE, 2014: 16). Try asking the class to make up their own rules and mnemonics. Maybe they have to help an alien to learn to read and write English, or they could make their own video clips or songs to help themselves and others understand and remember the rules and conventions.

Mathematics

- Finding patterns in sequences of numbers or the results of calculations, making a generalised statement from individual observations, experimenting with new methods of calculation or problem solving. (Generating new ideas.)
- Problem solving and investigations will probably involve children in applying known skills and ideas in different contexts, taking other people's ideas or starting points and moving them on or personalising them, putting different or disparate ideas together to make something new, and working towards a goal or set of goals.
- Choose a 'number of the week' every week and ask the children not only to share what they know about that number in mathematical contexts but also to refer to other cultural and everyday contexts. (See *Numbers: Facts, Figures and Fiction* by Richard Phillips [Badsey, 2004] for lots of excellent examples). (Applying known skills and ideas in different contexts.)

Science

- Whilst involved in examining evidence from scientific investigations children will be making generalised statements from individual observations and drawing conclusions from evidence. (Generating new ideas.)

- Children may have real-life experience that they can apply to scientific thinking and vice versa, particularly in how different materials behave and in reversible and irreversible changes. (Applying known skills and ideas in different contexts.)
- Children can be asked to demonstrate their knowledge of scientific principles through varied media, e.g. can they use movement to demonstrate the action of molecules in solids, liquids and gases, or the oxygenation of blood in the human body? (Communicating ideas in interesting or varied ways.)

Art and Design

- Examining and practising the techniques of 'masters' before using and perhaps adapting these in creating a new work. (Taking other people's ideas or starting points and moving them on or personalising them.)
- Using drawing, painting and sculpture to express their ideas and experiences. (Communicating ideas in interesting or varied ways.)
- Designing, planning and carrying out their own compositions or generating their own designs based on ideas and practice from their sketchbooks and skills work. (Generating new ideas, applying known skills and ideas in different contexts, putting different or disparate ideas together to make something new, working towards a goal or set of goals.)

Computing

- In creating their own programs children will be generating new ideas, applying known skills and ideas in different contexts, putting different or disparate ideas together to make something new, and working towards a goal or set of goals.
- Choosing and using a range of software to analyse data and communicate information appropriately to different audiences. (Communicating ideas in interesting or varied ways.)
- Creating an animation based on another part of the curriculum. (Generating new ideas, applying known skills and ideas in different contexts, communicating ideas in interesting or varied ways, putting different or disparate ideas together to make something new, working towards a goal or set of goals.)

Design & technology

- Designing an object, a system or a recipe. (Generating new ideas.)
- Using features or textures observed in the natural world or other contexts in a design, e.g. observing mini-beasts might lead to applying the way they move to the way a moving vehicle is designed and features of their

appearance might be used to design a suit of clothes. (Applying known skills and ideas in different contexts.)
- Designing a dish that incorporates food from two different cultures. (Putting different or disparate ideas together to make something new.)

Geography

- Using storytelling and writing to put learning in creative contexts and communicate information and what has been learned in varied ways, e.g. marking two points on a map and telling the story of a journey from one point to the other, using the map information for the setting but generating characters, plot etc. Making a map from a story e.g. *Rosie's Walk* by Pat Hutchins (Bodley Head, 1998) or *Each Peach Pear Plum* by Janet and Allan Ahlberg (Puffin, 1999). (Communicating ideas in interesting or varied ways.)
- Make contact with a school in another part of the country or the world and share information about your locality. This will involve having a specific goal and motivation for work on the locality and also not only collecting data and information but also deciding what is important, which questions to ask, comparing and analysing etc. (Generating new ideas.)

History

- Drawing conclusions from evidence. (Generating new ideas.)
- Communicating ideas and information in interesting or varied ways, e.g. by making a model, writing a story set in a particular period, acting a scene set in a particular place and time, creating a story or drama based on a historical picture or newspaper account. (This will also be putting different or disparate ideas together to make something new.)

Languages

- Put the learning in creative contexts and communicate information and what has been learned in varied ways by, e.g. inventing a character who needs the children's help but only speaks the language being learned. (Communicating ideas in interesting or varied ways, working towards a goal or set of goals.)
- Ask the children to invent games that will help them learn vocabulary or grammar. (Generating new ideas, applying known skills and ideas in different contexts, communicating ideas in interesting or varied ways, putting different or disparate ideas together to make something new, working towards a goal or set of goals.)

Music

- Composing a melody. (Generating new ideas.)
- Examining and practising the techniques of 'masters' before using and perhaps adapting these in creating a new work. (Taking other people's ideas or starting points and moving them on or personalising them.)
- Composing fusion music combining two different genres. (Putting different or disparate ideas together to make something new.)
- Composing music or writing songs for a particular occasion or as a soundtrack to an animation or existing short film clip. (Working towards a goal or set of goals.)

Physical Education

- Inventing and practising ways of moving differently. (Generating new ideas.)
- Applying the way machines, creatures or elements of the natural world move to a dance. (Applying known skills and ideas in different contexts.)
- Inventing, practising and applying tactics to a team or individual game. (Generating new ideas.)

Planning in two or more subjects

Here is an example of planning in two parallel subjects – geography and English. It is probably more a sequence of activities than one lesson and could be run during one day or, more likely, across two or more days.

 Classroom idea

Geography, English

Planning with parallel learning objectives

The activity is designed for 9 and 10 year olds but could be easily adapted for use with older or younger children.
    The learning objectives are:
Geography

- To ask geographical questions.
- To collect and record evidence.
- To communicate in ways appropriate to the task and audience.

(Continued)

(Continued)

- To use secondary sources of information.
- To identify and describe what places are like.
- To describe where places are.

Thinking skills

- To organise, generalise and categorise.

English

- To take notes.
- To understand the features of non-chronological texts including paragraphs and the use of sub-headings.

The activities go like this:

1 (a) Introduce the children to the idea of note taking, why it is useful, how it differs from writing in full sentences, what abbreviations are etc.
  (b) Provide the children with good quality, uncaptioned pictures of the place you are going to study. Ask the children to work in pairs to discuss what they can see in the pictures, what the countryside looks like, what they can see people doing, what they think the climate is like etc. The learning question is: What can I deduce about a place from photographs? Or, more simply: What is this place like?
  (c) Ask the children to take it in turns to write notes on a sticky note about what they have discovered from the pictures. Each new point should be on a different sticky note.
2 Repeat the above activity using different sources of information or combine the sources for older, more able children.
3 Ask the children what they have discovered and which heading that might go under. Introduce them to the idea of categories. If they saw people picking olives, that might go under 'Food and Drink' or it might go under 'Industry'. Discuss the nature of categories. Ask the children in pairs or small groups to draw up a list of categories that might be useful with the information they have found out.
4 Ask the children to group their sticky notes under their chosen category headings. At this point, discuss how well the categories worked. Did they have information that fitted into more than one? What would they do about that? Could they combine any categories? What difference would that make etc.? If necessary, this might be the time to combine information from different groups or to do some more research if they have discovered categories with very little information.

5   Explain that they are going to write up what they have discovered about the place. Revisit, if necessary, the nature of non-fiction texts. This account is going to be organised into the categories they have chosen. Each category will be one paragraph. If necessary, unpick why this is useful to a reader, how the paragraphs are set out, etc. Look at a range of different non-fiction texts and discuss why sub-headings are used. Ask the children to use their notes to write up in full what they have discovered. Let them choose whether to use sub-headings or not for their paragraphs.

As can be seen from this outline, there is learning in more than one subject area. In some schools the activities might flow naturally without the necessity for designating a particular 'English lesson' or 'geography lesson', but these would work just as well if particular lessons were 'ring fenced' as long as the children realised that their thinking and learning was not curtailed by the designations.

It may seem trivial, but a different approach to 'subject-specific' planning can raise many practical questions. Teachers will often ask how they can organise the use of exercise books. Do they need to use specific English books if a lot of writing in different subjects is to happen in these? What do they do if subject coordinators want to see their work in a particular subject and it is spread over different books? This is obviously something that schools need to discuss and reach decisions about for themselves, but many that are working on a more integrated approach have books or folders with a 'theme' or 'topic' title and all work under that heading is done in there. Obviously a folder, although potentially more difficult for children to keep organised, means that individual pieces of work can be taken out for sampling if necessary. Keeping a folder organised requires specific time and input and support from the teacher, but perhaps this is time well spent – keeping organised folders is a very useful life skill!

The ideas given so far have been deliberately chosen within fairly traditional parameters, and have been more to do with taking already existing learning objectives and lesson ideas and putting them within a context that encourages links and connections, wider choice and autonomy for the children, and within relevant contexts. Previous chapters will have introduced you to many other facets of creativity and we will now consider how to plan for these.

Guy Claxton comments, 'Schools have often been preoccupied with the kind of learning in which you are trying to get to a clearly defined goal. But not all learning is like that' (Claxton, 2002: 32). He goes on to outline how sometimes better work emerges if a student is unsure at the start just where they are going with a piece of work.

Let us consider the learning around the distant place in the previous activity. This was allied with very clear learning about note taking and organising non-chronological writing. These are both things that need to be understood, will be extremely useful, and have life-long applications. So the question is not 'what can we do instead?', but 'what can we do as well?'

It might be worth encouraging the children to develop and express their personal responses to the research they have done about the place they have been studying in geography. This could happen in a variety of ways, not just in writing, and even if the written word is the child's chosen medium they have the choice of many different genres. Just telling the class they can choose any medium to communicate ideas about the country is likely to be far too broad a choice for most children. The activity needs to be broken down to encourage them to develop personal responses to the subject matter and see the possibilities for communicating their ideas in different ways.

A first activity might be to ask the children to list three things that made them feel they would really like to go to that place and three things that would make them think twice about going. Then they could list three things that mystified them or they need to find out more about and three things they would most like to do if they went there. Listing activities or ranking features in order using certain criteria is a really good way to encourage children to recall and select features and develop opinions, and lists both ranked and unranked seem to fascinate people as can be seen from the television programmes and internet sites developed around them. Sharing a list or ranking will allow children to begin to debate and justify their views: 'I put that one much higher up because .. ', 'I didn't think of that but you're right, it should definitely be on the list.'

You could use drama to mime the various activities the children saw in their research and build still pictures/tableaux of significant activities in a 'day in the life of' different inhabitants. Different movement or dance elements could be explored to represent moving in the climate and terrain.

Ethnic or regional fabric or architectural design features could be examined and described using five evocative words. Statistics relating to the country such as for the population, industry, exports, health or education could be examined, and the children asked to look for patterns or use them to generate questions.

All of these could be quite short activities, designed not to provide exhaustive answers or finished pieces of work but to open up avenues that the children might find it interesting to explore further. During the activities the class could be encouraged to think which approaches or ideas they find most appealing or interesting and which questions might be emerging that they would like to explore in more detail. Then a day or two half-days, for example, could be allocated for them to pursue their ideas individually or in groups, and to share their outcomes in appropriate ways.

Personal thought and reflection

If you were in the class that had undertaken the above activities (but as the adult you are now) what would you most have enjoyed exploring? What would you have chosen to develop and how would you have gone about it? What would the outcome have looked like?

   Now imagine each of the other possibilities you could have chosen – what would you have done if you had pursued those ideas? Which media would you have worked in? Although you will be planning activities for children, most primary teachers get a real 'buzz' from some activities and wish they could be doing them too; some actually do work at an activity at their own level on occasions. The excitement of thinking 'I would love to do that' can be a good indication that you have planned an engaging activity. Reflect on the activities you have planned, taught or observed that have given you this feeling. Were your feelings a good match for the children's enjoyment and interest?

Extending the range of the learning opportunities in this way will now give opportunities for the children to develop their creativity by allowing them to:

- generate new ideas;
- apply known skills and ideas in different contexts;
- take other people's ideas or starting points and move these on or personalise them;
- communicate ideas in interesting or varied ways;
- put different or disparate ideas together to make something new;
- work towards a goal or set of goals;
- evaluate their own or others' work;
- adapt and improve on their work in light of their own or others' evaluations.

As will be seen, all the key elements of creativity are possible outcomes of the extra activity although not every child will necessarily demonstrate all of these.

   In addition, the following geography outcomes will probably be met in addition to the ones outlined earlier:

- To analyse evidence and draw conclusions.
- To identify and explain the different views that people, including themselves, hold about topical geographical issues.
- To describe and explain how and why places are similar to and different from other places in the same country and elsewhere in the world.

Other things to consider

In both the above examples the elements that would potentially give rise to the most creative outcomes were additions to a more traditionally focused activity. Harvard professor David Perkins talks about 'tame topics' and 'wild topics' (quoted in Claxton, 2002: 85), but any topic can be given its wild side if it is offered to the children in ways they can investigate and explore without too much of a predetermined path and outcomes. As with most things, it is a matter of balance.

There follow some suggestions of considerations or activities which you might think about when planning activities with more creative outcomes. These are in addition to the many suggestions in previous chapters. The references will lead you to the sources of the ideas and more detailed analysis and discussion:

- Are you offering opportunities for the children to be creative both individually and in group situations? Are they making contact with people with different ideas beyond their own class or year group? Ken Robinson makes the point, 'We are laced together in networks of knowledge ... The creativity of a culture depends on how open these networks are and how easily we can access the knowledge of other people' (2001: 169).
- Are you offering opportunities to learn the skills of being creative as well as opportunities to use them? As we saw in previous chapters the children cannot be expected to be able to work creatively without developing appropriate skills. Lessons or activities developing relevant skills may need to be planned discretely. This implies that it will be necessary to assess the children's needs and abilities in different aspects of being creative in order to provide the learning opportunities they will need when appropriate. This is developed in more detail in the next chapter.
- 'Can you impart information in a way that suggests there are genuine alternatives? Can you teach routines ... as something that had to be imaginatively worked out and can you encourage the child to reflect on possible alternatives to them?' (Passmore, 1980: 162, quoted in Craft, 2000). Much in creativity is about seeing alternatives so try asking the children to look for alternative uses for everyday objects or alternative actions for characters in books (Craft et al., 2008: 90, 93).
- Can you cope with messiness at times? Creative working can often be a messy procedure. This is not just in terms of materials (in fact this might not be the case at all) but also in terms of thinking and doing. People involved in creative work may pursue one idea and then discard this to pick up something else; they may not work in logical stages (for example generating ideas and trying them out without formal design stages) or they may seem to be following two ideas at once (Craft, 2000: 96). This will be

a balancing act between structure and fluidity and you will have to decide whether all the children in your classroom have to conform to the same constraints all the time. If children know when neat presentation is important and when you are looking for ideas and methods they will be able to understand your expectations. You will need to be clear with explanations of what you are looking for at any particular time, and encourage the class to talk about their working processes with you in order that you can advise them about how to proceed in ways that will help them individually to refine their working methods.

- Can you offer inspiring resources, on occasion, that will stimulate the children's ideas? This may be in terms of technology that will inspire different approaches such as digital cameras, movie cameras, voting pods or good quality pictures provided for research. It may be resources such as fabric or leather or wood that they can use. Although good resources do not automatically lead to high quality work they can make a significant impact, as can the ease of access by the children (HMI, 2003).

Creative assessment

Assessing children's learning in both formative and summative ways is essential to good teaching. There is no reason, however, that the assessment process should not be as creative as any other aspect of your teaching.

Dylan Wiliam has long been at the forefront of championing effective assessment and many of the ideas he promoted are now standard fare in primary classrooms. Your school may have the materials *Embedding formative assessment: a two-year professional development pack* by Dylan Wiliam and Siobhan Leahy (Leahy and Wiliam, 2013). In this pack are many ideas for formative assessment, particularly in relation to marking and feedback. For example, with older pupils you could try giving a group of four children slips of paper with the feedback comments about their work on, mixed up and unnamed. They will have to read the comments and work out which comments refer to which piece of work. Another of their useful creative ideas that is particularly good for maths is not to mark answers right or wrong, but to tell a child how many of their answers are wrong and give them time in class to try and find which those are and correct their mistakes.

Devising an activity that gives you evidence of what the children have learned and understood can be a creative activity for a teacher. It involves looking back at what you were specifically planning (and hoping!) that the children would learn, and devising an activity to test whether that learning had taken place. It is important to remember that some children may find it difficult to communicate the depth of their learning in written words, so some assessment activities might involve making models, acting out situations, or drawing.

Classroom example

History

After a history study unit looking at changes in the local area in Victorian times, the teacher wanted to know if the children had understood what changes had taken place, the reasons for the changes, and the results of those changes. She also wanted to know if they had recognised that while some things had changed other things had stayed the same. She devised a work-sheet with four outline faces which the children could personalise as Victorian people. Each one had a large speech bubble next to it. The first speech bubble said 'I built my house here because … ', the second said, 'You wouldn't believe how this area has changed. Once it was … Now it is …'. The final two speech bubbles said, 'The good things about the changes are … ' and 'The bad things about the changes are … '. A final space below said 'But some things stayed the same … '.

This worksheet gave the children the chance to reflect individually on what they had learned and then communicate that to the teacher in a way that gave her information not only about their factual recall but also about their deduc-tive capabilities in areas that were specifically important to history. For children who might have had difficulty writing their answers the speech bubbles gave a perfect vehicle by which to rehearse and actually speak their responses.

Sometimes you can plan an activity that gives you assessment information in more than one subject.

 Classroom idea

Geography, English

Give the children a map of an area with interesting features. This can vary in complexity according to their map-reading ability. Ask the class to mark two points (A and B) on opposite sides of the map. They must imagine a reason that a character has to travel from point A to point B. What genre of story will this be? Historical, science fiction, adventure, for young children? Their task is to write part of a story that describes the journey from point A to point B. They must make the genre totally clear to the reader from the opening paragraph and throughout the piece.

This activity will give the teacher information not only about each child's narrative ability and knowledge of the features of different genres, but also about their ability to read a map accurately and visualise and interpret geographic features.

Chapter summary

This chapter has considered planning for creative outcomes in individual lessons. It suggested starting from lessons planned without particular intentions to encourage creativity, and then using the key elements of creativity and what we know so far about contexts that encourage and foster creativity, finding ways to incorporate these within the lesson or as extensions to the lesson. It highlighted additional considerations from research and pointed out the necessity of keeping a balance between developing skills in working creatively and opportunities to practise those skills in creative contexts. It also looked at possible areas where creativity could be found in individual subjects and how it was possible to devise creative ways to assess learning.

 Further study

Critical reflection: Activity 7

Allow an hour for this activity.

Choose one subject that you would like to teach more creatively. *Identify* what you think you already do well while teaching this. *Synthesise* your evidence.

Identify any of the relevant creative characteristics that you want to try out in the next few lessons of this subject. Prioritise one and adapt your lesson plans accordingly.

Decide how you are going to *evaluate* this adaptation. Plan how and when you are going to complete the evaluation. You may want to discuss this change with a colleague. You could request a lesson observation to be done while you are teaching one of your adapted plans so that you can have a richer discussion with the person who has witnessed the lesson.

Evaluate your learning from this change. Try to *view the change from the children's perspective*. What differences will they have experienced? How did this affect their learning, behaviour and engagement?

 Further reading

Phillips, R. (2004) *Numbers: Facts, Figures and Fiction*, 2nd edn. Evesham: Badsey.

Jeffrey, R. (2008) 'Creative learning identities', *Education 3–13*, 36 (3): 253–63.

Wegerif, R. (2010) *Mind Expanding: Teaching for Thinking and Creativity in Primary Education*. Abingdon: Routledge.

CHAPTER 8

MEDIUM-TERM PLANNING FOR CREATIVE OUTCOMES

 Learning objectives in this chapter:

To consider the different elements that are essential in creating a medium-term plan that will encourage and foster creativity in children, including:

- The needs and interests of the children
- The areas of learning specified for that academic year
- The values that underpin the curriculum
- The context within which the learning could occur
- The balance of knowledge and application
- The pace and flow across a term or half-term, where subjects can be 'blocked'
- Where links can be made and what should stay discrete
- How creativity can be assessed

Relevant Teachers' Standards for this chapter

A teacher must:

1   **Set high expectations which inspire, motivate and challenge pupils**

1c   demonstrate consistently the positive attitudes, values and behaviour which are expected of pupils

4	**Plan and teach well structured lessons**
4e	contribute to the design and provision of an engaging curriculum within the relevant subject area(s)
8	**Fulfil wider professional responsibilities**
8a	make a positive contribution to the wider life and ethos of the school

We have now come to the point of putting together all the elements outlined in previous chapters to be able to plan a cohesive and coherent learning experience for the children across a half-term or a term. Sometimes there may even be the possibility of seeing links and progression across the whole school year. Some schools will call each unit a scheme of work, some a medium-term plan or termly plan. We will call it a unit of work.

Planning at this level has become, in recent years, something of a dying art in many schools. Medium-term plans will often have been drawn up some years previously and are then given to the year group teacher to follow year on year. Some schools will expect this to be done without alteration while others will expect teachers to personalise the plans. The introduction of the new National Curriculum in September 2014 led most schools to reconsider their planning, but many have tried to change as little as possible whilst 'tweaking' for new requirements in some subjects.

When thinking about planning in more creative ways and for more crea-tive outcomes many teachers will ask whether this will cause them much more work. The honest answer here is that when compared with just picking up a plan prepared by someone else it will, and particularly in the short term as a teacher gets used to planning in this way and builds up their experience of the various activities and methods that work well. However, while this may prove more time-consuming to begin with, it will be considerably more satisfying for both the teacher and their class. Planning for creative outcomes is a creative activity in its own right and can give teachers just as much of a 'buzz' as being part of the activity in the classroom.

There has been a considerable amount of discussion in recent years con-cerning the balance of 'skills' and 'knowledge' in the curriculum. Alexander (2010) argues that the term 'skills' needs to be used with more discrimination by educators and comments, 'though the generic skills approach purports to address the claims of lifelong learning, it actually sells such learning short, for it elevates being able to do something over knowing, understanding, reflecting, speculating, analysing and evaluating which arguably are no less essential to the fulfilled, successful and useful life'. He defines knowledge as 'the process and outcome of coming to know, or the combination of what is known and how such knowledge is acquired. It encompasses knowledge both propositional and procedural, and both public and personal, and it allows for reservation and scepticism as well as certainty' (Alexander, 2010: 250, 251). John Hattie, in *Visible Learning*, which synthesises thousands of research findings, concludes that 'training, practice and encouragement in using creative thinking skills can improve an individual's ability to use creative thinking techniques such as thinking with fluency, flexibility, and with an element of the unusual in response to questions or problems' (Hattie, 2009: 155). He concludes that planned and deliberate learning of these skills has a marked effect on attainment. During the planning phase of the new National Curriculum there was much discussion of the influence of the educational theories of E.D. Hirsch (see, for example Hirsch, 1996) and the phrase 'core knowledge' was used frequently. This phrase is generally applied to factual knowledge. Hirsch's theories are actually more complex than they are often characterised and some commentators are doubtful as to how they transfer from their American roots.

However you apply the definitions or take sides in the debate, it seems obvious that learning involves learning how to do things as well as purely factual knowledge and that factual knowledge needs to be applied and used. The planning of learning experiences that we provide for children will need to have a balance of these elements; it will have to include the subject-specific knowledge and skills (including those needed to be creative) but within contexts that will allow children to apply their knowledge in ways that will engage, challenge and require them to think and innovate.

 Personal thought and reflection

What would your definition of 'knowledge' be? What does it take to be a knowledgeable person? Does knowing lots of general knowledge make you well educated? What else is necessary? How good do you think the balance of knowledge and skills has been in the schools you have been in?

When planning a unit of work we are seldom starting with a blank sheet. This is actually helpful. There are already certain fixed points that we have to take into consideration but even these give us scope to question and make decisions. They can be considered under these four overarching questions.

1 What are the children's needs and interests?

All classes are different. A class of 8 year olds in one school may have many similarities with a similar aged class in another school but there will be many differences too. The area the school is in, the community it serves, the gender balance, the particular learning needs of the children, not to mention the fact that they are all individuals with different ideas, talents and interests, will make every class individual. So, even if working from an existing plan, a teacher would want to adapt it to the particular needs and interests of the class in order to make it relevant to them.

Most teachers start a new school year with 'getting to know you' activities, and in Chapter 4 we looked at some designed to encourage children to get to know and trust each other. These can also be used to identify particular types of books the children enjoy, or favourite hobbies and activities in and outside school, and can help steer you towards the contexts for learning that the children might find most stimulating.

In the section on Pupil Voice in Chapter 4 we looked at how we could consult children on what they wanted to know within a particular topic or how we could note and incorporate other areas of interest. This is sometimes called curriculum co-construction, although in primary schools it is probably more like curriculum consultation. If this is to be in any way meaningful, though, it is worth remembering what was said in Chapter 4 about using questioning and discussion to extend the children's expectations beyond what they already know about a subject and to excite their curiosity to enquire beyond what they expect. Children can be very quick to establish their own boundaries based on prior knowledge and expectations. In the previous chapter it was explained how, before asking them to choose an area for open-ended personal investigation, it was advisable to give them 'taster' ideas and experiences, and the same idea would be useful when involving the children in devising a unit of work. This process was found to be most successful with secondary school music students. In the evaluation of the *Musical Futures* project they noted, 'consultation can be most effective when students have something to base their experiences on' (www.musicalfutures. org.uk/resource/27349). This can and should be an ongoing activity as you will find new areas opening up for you and the children as you progress.

The children's needs will also have to be taken into consideration. This will include the particular learning needs of individuals, their social and emotional needs, and also their needs as creative individuals. We have already established that children cannot be creative or learn in creative ways without certain skills and attributes. In order to provide appropriate learning experiences for your class it will be necessary to assess what they can already do in the realm of creativity and therefore what they need to learn, in the same way that any assessment for learning would be used. The assessment proforma on the following page may prove useful here.

 ## Individual activity

Use the grid offered here when teaching or observing a lesson with potential creative outcomes. Which children can you observe showing which aspects of creativity? Over the class as a whole, are particular aspects more fully developed than others? Did the activity tend to display some aspects rather than others?

How could you use the grid to aid planning for individuals, groups and the whole class? Try using the grid in lessons in different subject areas. Are the aspects of creativity applicable to any subject area? Could they be?

Children who can ...	Names	Evidence
generate new ideas		
apply known skills and ideas in different contexts		
take other people's ideas or starting points and move them on or personalise them		
communicate ideas in interesting or varied ways		
put different or disparate ideas together to make something new		
work towards a goal or set of goals		
evaluate their own and others' work		
adapt and improve on their work in the light of their own or others' evaluations		
Implications for future planning:		

2 What is in your curriculum for the year?

Most teachers are given details of what topics under which subject areas should be taught in each term. Whether you can move particular topics from term to term will probably depend on whether your school has parallel year groups, and if so, whether you are adapting your planning as a team. The most helpful situation is one where you undertake to cover all the topics in particular subjects during the academic year, but have the freedom and flexibility to move things from one term to another if it would make for better links and connections, tie in with outside events, or make for better progression for your class in a different order.

To make such decisions, it would be useful at this stage to think which topics within which subjects seem to have natural links that could prove useful in planning and make sure these appear in the same term.

Even if the content of each term has to stay the same, there is still plenty of scope for tailoring the learning provision to the children's needs and interests.

3 What do you consider to be at the 'heart' of the curriculum for the term? (What is most important? What do you want to say?)

This is really the key question. There is factual knowledge the children need to acquire, there are key concepts and core skills they need to develop, but there is a range of ways these can be taught, a huge choice of contexts in which the learning could happen, and often different viewpoints that can be encouraged.

 Classroom example

History

As is the case with many teachers, a teacher with a class of 6 and 7 year olds was given the important historical figure, Florence Nightingale, to study with her class. While she understood that Florence Nightingale's life story was iconic in British history, the teacher felt that her class also needed role models that were not white and upper class. She therefore decided to complement Florence Nightingale's story with that of Mary Seacole. This provided a different perspective to the children's learning; they studied the prejudices that both women encountered and their need for persistence and determination. This put the learning about the Crimean War firmly in the context of the British Empire and allowed these particular children to relate to the story of a woman from Jamaica who made a real difference to people's lives.

This choice fulfilled identified needs for the children and upheld the values of the school.

The above simple example shows the importance of considering the context and inherent values of what is taught. Factual knowledge occurs within a context that is influenced by many factors and can be subject to interpretation and bias. Jonathan Barnes puts the situation clearly: 'Values – the fundamental beliefs that guide all action – are particularly reflected in the curriculum a school offers. *Curriculum* ... is defined very broadly to include not just the subjects taught, but also the choices made within those subjects, the styles and means chosen to teach them, the activities, attitudes, environments, relationships and beliefs that pervade a school' (Barnes, 2015: 19).

Of all subjects, history is probably the most open to interpretation, but the examples chosen of musicians, authors, scientists and artists carry their own agenda, as do themes and countries studied in geography or the importance given to PSHE. Teachers will need to balance what they know of the needs of the children, the school's values and those of the local community in order to make decisions about the choices they must make.

 Individual activity

Look through the topics in a school's medium-term plans. What interpretations could these imply? What would be the benefits and drawbacks of each interpretation? Would these vary according to a child's age and ability? What other considerations are relevant when interpreting a topic for a particular group of children?
Examples:

- The Roman Empire and its impact on Britain: we could emphasise the amazing technology and organisation of the Romans in a 'what they did for us' interpretation. We could focus on the pre-existing Celtic society to understand that there are losses as well as gains when a country is invaded and settled.
- Human geography: we could look at world issues such as trade links and the distribution of natural resources. We could emphasise our impact on the world as consumers. We could focus on small-scale projects that the children can influence directly, looking at their impact on the local environment.

Apply the questions above to these examples, adding different interpretations to those given if applicable, and then continue with other topics.

Many teachers make selections of content and interpretation without recognising the impact that these have on what is actually learned. Becoming alert to possible different interpretations and making choices after consideration of the implications are important. This applies to all aspects and choices, from resources and visual images used, to teaching methods and selection of content.

4 What context will make the learning coherent?

We have already explored what we mean by 'authentic contexts' in Chapter 6. Setting the learning within a context that is relevant to the children and that motivates them is likely to make that learning deeper and more memorable (see Lave and Wenger, 1991). It is likely that there are also possibilities for making links and connections to other curriculum subjects and for the learning to happen within a cross-curricular context. The issue of cross-curricular planning is looked at in more detail later on in this chapter.

Sometimes the context for the learning will appear obvious from the outset, but sometimes the curriculum content will seem like a disparate collection of items with very little cohesion. This is the time to 'play around' with different ideas and see where they take you (applying the creative process yourself to the planning activity).

The first thing to try is probably whether there is a particular story or poem that has links with any of the prescribed content and that the children would love. Basing a unit of work around a powerful text produces benefits in many areas. As English generally has a large time allocation the children benefit by linking other areas of learning to the text being studied, and the emotional connection and empathy for characters and their dilemmas that a story generates can motivate them to explore issues and find out more about the background to the story.

 Classroom example

Cross-curricular

In a class of 7 year olds (Year 2) the curriculum content for the Spring term included:

- uses of everyday materials in science;
- a Design & Technology unit on textiles involving sewing a glove puppet;
- an English unit on different stories by the same author;
- the SEAL unit 'Good to Be Me'.

The teacher 'played' with ideas related to these topics. These aspects seemed relevant:

- Textiles are materials themselves. There are many different types and they have different properties.
- The D&T unit's learning objectives are about joining textiles by sewing. It doesn't have to be a puppet.
- The SEAL unit contains activities looking at worries.

It was the connection to worries that first triggered a mental link to the book *Dogger* by Shirley Hughes (Red Fox, 1997). In the story, Dave has a toy dog called Dogger that he takes to bed with him. Without it he cannot sleep. When he loses the toy he is distraught. Dogger ends up on a stall at the school fair and is bought by a little girl who will not give him up. Dave's big sister, Bella, eventually persuades the little girl to swap Dogger for the giant teddy she has won in the sports day races.

(Continued)

(Continued)

Immediately certain connections and possibilities began to occur:

- Shirley Hughes has written many popular books for the age range.
- *Dogger* introduces themes such as an older sibling helping a younger, why we often take a toy to bed with us, and why worries may seem worse at bedtime.
- Toys are made of different materials. What properties of the materials make them suitable for different sorts of toys?

This led to planning a unit of work that investigated the properties of materials with specific relevance to whether they were suitable for using for toys and the particular properties of items that 'soothe' or make us feel better. Children were allowed to relate this to when they were younger and may have had a piece of blanket or other comforter, but they were also encouraged to 'admit' to still liking to take a toy to bed and discuss why. Activities concerning issues about worries and how you could deal with them were planned. Shirley Hughes was chosen as a significant author and a selection of her books were read and aspects of the style, story content etc. were identified. The children conducted a survey about bedtime toys and their properties, and then designed, made and evaluated a suitable toy for themselves or a younger child that would help that child feel safe and not worry.

 Individual activity

Using the above classroom example, which elements would offer the potential for creativity by the children? Use the chart in Chapter 7 to help you.

Next stages in planning

Considering these four overarching questions (What are the children's needs and interests? What is in your curriculum for the year? What do you consider to be at the 'heart' of the curriculum for the term? What context will make the learning coherent?) should lead to an understanding of which areas of the curriculum will be linked by this context and what will need to be taught discretely. The chart given below might be useful at this stage of planning.

When creating a coherent plan for a term or half-term it is important to both prioritise and provide balance. It is impossible to address everything you would want to within the time available in a school day, week or term. You will have to select and the questions given in the chart should help you to make that selection.

Your first task is to decide which areas within a topic you want to focus on, what 'slant' you want to take (Question 1). Taking the needs and interests

Questions for curriculum planning

1 What do I want the children to understand about the topic by the end? (Why is it important? What values will be inherent in it? What knowledge, concepts and skills will be developed?)

2 What specific needs or interests do this class have that I should take into consideration? How will I make it relevant to them?

3 What 'top three' priority questions do I want them to investigate? (key questions)

4 What will the best opportunities be for:

   i Creativity? (generating new ideas, combining different ideas, communicating in interesting or varied ways etc.)

   ii Enquiry-based learning and problem solving?

   iii Involving other adults?

   iv Involving the children in planning?

   v Using computing creatively?

   vi Using space and groupings flexibly?

   vii Learning in 'hands-on' ways?

5 What is the best order for things to happen in? (pacing grid)

6 Are all areas/subjects equally important? Is anything 'light touch' this term/half-term? What will link and what will be discrete?

7 What will my learning objectives be? (session planning)

of the children into consideration what context will you place the learning in and how will you make it relevant to them (Question 2)? This might give you an overarching learning question or a title for the unit of work.

 Classroom example

Cross-curricular

In a class of 11 year olds (Year 6) in the Spring term the teachers felt bound to spend considerable time preparing the children for their SATs tests. The children were unmotivated by this; they liked a more exciting, practical approach. The teachers decided to base their term's planning around the book *Stormbreaker* by Anthony Horowitz (Walker Books, 2000). Their classroom would become a spy school, training new spies. They would need to learn lots of maths and science to use on their missions. They made 'training passports' which itemised what they needed to know, and when they had passed each task, test or assessment their passport was stamped. Drama was used to simulate their training assignments and writing in different genres was generated by these sessions. Both staff and children loved this new approach. They called the topic 'Spy School'.

Many teachers find using a mental map or 'spider diagram' useful at this stage of planning. With the title or central question in the centre of an A3 piece of paper you can visually mark in which elements would link and connect to this context and which areas will stay outside, taught discretely. You might even find that some of the subject areas left outside actually link well together to form a 'mini topic' that could run alongside or go after the main unit of work.

You should then be ready to generate the three priority questions you want the children to investigate (Question 3). This will give you the outline for what is to be included and what might be held in reserve. Having reached this stage, you can begin to 'pace' the progression of the unit of work. Many teachers only plan week by week and have no real sense of where the unit of work is going. It is important, even if some of the areas are open-ended, to have a sense of the shape of the unit, rather like a story map, to see where it is leading and therefore, for example, what knowledge, concepts and skills need to be learned and practised early on so they can be used later.

Questions 4, 5 and 6 all interrelate at this stage. In 'pacing out' the structure of the unit across the term or half-term you will be deciding which areas of learning need to happen before or after others. You will also need to decide which aspects will work best with a weekly session, allowing time for reflection, and which could be 'blocked', perhaps spending every afternoon for a week on a particular activity. Some of these decisions may be based on practical considerations; many teachers will choose to 'block' their D&T work, for example, so that resources can be kept readily available and projects do not have to be put away and stored between sessions.

This is the time when you can decide on the creative focus for your unit of work. Which creative aspect do you want the children to focus on? Do you want them to generate new ideas or more creative ways of communicating ideas? Do you want them to ask more searching questions for themselves or be able to plan ways to investigate those questions? Do you want to encourage creative writing or dance or design? This will involve a consideration of Question 2 again, an assessment of what they have already achieved and what they need to develop next.

When the outline has been 'paced' across the available weeks and specific activities allocated to particular weeks to provide suitable progression, then weekly and session planning can begin.

Issues in more depth

The above outline of the planning process will have brought to the fore some issues that have yet to be considered. This next section will look at some of those in more detail.

The first of these is **Values**. The Curriculum 2000 (published in 1999) both begins and ends with a consideration of values. It starts with a section on values, aims and purposes which states 'Education influences and reflects the values of society, and the kind of society we want to be. It is important, therefore, to recognise a broad set of common values and purposes that underpin the school curriculum and the work of schools' (DfEE/QCA, 1999: 10). The final section of the National Curriculum handbook consists of a statement of values in education and the community. This is offered so that schools can 'base their teaching and the school ethos on these values' (1999: 147).

 Individual activity

Look at the statements of values at the beginning and end of the National Curriculum handbook for primary teachers (DfEE/QCA, 1999). Do you feel that these values are still relevant for schools? How do schools you know promote these values (a) in their ethos, practices and methodologies, (b) in their curriculum?

Now look at the new National Curriculum (DfE, 2014). Are any underpinning values explicit? Do you feel any are implicit? If so, which values are these and where are they to be found? How are they similar to or different from the previous National Curriculum?

Do you feel schools should have their own values stated explicitly?

It is important not only for your individual planning to exemplify and promote the school's values but also for you as a teacher to have a firm and coherent set of values yourself. Professional values have always been a crucial part of a teacher's competencies, underpinning all of their interactions with parents, colleagues and children, but these are often overlooked in their planning. Jonathan Barnes argues that an ongoing discussion of values should be part of every school community, and offers the following list of questions to be considered (2015: 208):

- What is education for?
- What is our attitude to children?
- How should adults behave towards children?
- What kind of children do we want our children to be?
- What kind of adults do we want our children to become?
- What kind of education do we want our children to have?
- What kind of education do *children* want to have?
- What are the most important issues for this community?
- What negative or unhelpful mindsets should we try to shift?
- What sustains, motivates and generates optimism in the school's adults?
- How can we build hope into children's lives through the curriculum?
- What things do we treasure most?

The impact of education on the future of individuals and society is clear within these questions. Barnes states, 'it is arguably the teacher's prime professional responsibility to be optimistic' (2015: 208). We have already discussed the importance of children finding relevance in what they learn, and this not only relates to them seeing a purpose in what they are learning and finding it interesting but also for them to learn well it has to really matter to them in ways that touch their emotions (Abbs, 2003: 14–15; Claxton, 2002: 21).

 Personal thought and reflection

- What examples have you noticed of schools' values being implicit in lesson planning? Where have you demonstrated your values in classroom organisation, interactions, or lesson planning?
- What examples have you noticed of children's emotions being engaged during learning experiences? Were these in particular subject areas or particular types of activity? If so, why do you think that is?

We should now consider the issue of **'cross-curricular' planning and learning**. This is a huge topic and a good start to understanding it in depth would be to read Jonathan Barnes's book *Cross-curricular Learning 3–14* (Barnes, 2015).

However, there are some points that can be considered now. The first is that, although in education we are accustomed to dividing knowledge into 'subjects', the world does not operate like that. Although some subjects can seem clear and defined, even in school curricula, there are often times when there are overlaps, and in the real world, re-tiling your bathroom doesn't immediately make you think 'this is maths, this is design, this is technology, this is science', although you are almost certainly using all of those subjects. Working in cross-curricular ways in school can help children find real-life relevance and application for their learning, and can also help them apply knowledge and skills learned in one area to another.

There are obviously difficulties in working in cross-curricular ways. Each subject has its own specialist knowledge, concepts and skills that need to be learned. It is all too easy to believe you are teaching two or more subjects when in fact the children are learning neither. Colouring in a printed picture of Elizabeth I is probably neither art nor history. So, it is important to be clear about what exactly your learning intentions are in any particular activity and in which subjects you actually intend learning to happen. This is not to say that learning will not happen in other areas too, but it is advisable to limit your planning to linking two or at most three subjects together at any one time.

Chapter summary

In this chapter we have looked at the important considerations that impact on planning a unit of work. We have identified four overarching questions:

- What are the children's needs and interests?
- What is in your curriculum for the year?
- What do you consider to be at the 'heart' of the curriculum for the term?
- What context will make the learning coherent?

We have examined issues of relevance and of making choices about the aspects of subjects that are presented. This led to a consideration of values in education. A proforma was included to use when planning to highlight the issues that need to be considered, and a suggestion for the chronological process of planning at this level. Some of the issues concerning cross-curricular planning and learning were also identified.

Further study

Critical reflection: Activity 8

Allow at least an hour for this activity.

Choose one or both of these enquiry questions depending on your interests and the time available.

- 'We mostly learn what is truly and personally relevant to us'. This is how Barnes explains Peter Abbs's theory of 'existential engagement' (Barnes, 2015: 208).

What other evidence do you have for the impact of the emotions on learning? What is meant by 'deep learning' and how does this link with theories of creativity? *Examine* the issues involved here. *Seek the framework or theoretical basis* that underpin these issues.

- Can creativity lead to individualism and a disregard for others? How can we educate students for 'wise creativity'? These issues are dealt with in the collection of essays published as *Creativity, Wisdom and Trusteeship* (Craft et al., 2008).

What impact do these considerations have on our planning and teaching? How do we address them?

Examine your personal reaction to these issues. What beliefs, assumptions, knowledge, attitudes and values do you bring to the issues? Try to *view the issues from various different perspectives*. How do these perspectives *challenge our original assumptions? Consider the consequences* of the issues raised.

 Further reading

Barnes, J. (2015) *Cross-Curricular Learning 3–14*, 3rd edn. London: Sage.
Hattie, J. (2009) *Visible Learning*. London: Routledge.
Lave, J. and Wenger, E. (1991) *Situated Learning*. Cambridge: Cambridge University Press.

CHAPTER 9

CASE STUDIES:
CREATIVITY IN PRACTICE

 Learning objectives in this chapter:

- To understand how the theories and ideas introduced in this book can be integrated into practice in the primary classroom
- To recognise aspects of creative teaching, creative learning and teaching to develop creativity within case studies of planning and teaching in primary schools

Relevant Teachers' Standards for this chapter

A teacher must:

4   Plan and teach well structured lessons

4e   contribute to the design and provision of an engaging curriculum within the relevant subject area(s)

In this chapter we will look at a series of case studies from different primary schools which illustrate elements of planning, teaching and learning creatively, and teaching to develop creativity in the children involved.

CASE STUDY 1

The Identity Project

Starting point

This was a cross-curricular project devised for a class of 10 and 11 year olds (Year 6) in South London. It came from a desire to help the children feel proud of who they were and what they had achieved so far and to feel ready for the transition to secondary school. It had as its background discussions in the news media about the pros and cons of 'multiculturalism', the nature of citizenship, and what it was to be British.

The starting point was two questions: 'How do I come to be living in South London at this time?' and 'What is my culture?'

The project spanned the entire year, with aspects linked to different subjects in different terms. Across the year it involved work in English, history, geography, the creative arts, PSHE, computing, and dance. Maths and science were generally taught discretely, but links and connections were made where relevant.

Much of this work was taught in partnership with a teacher whose specific role was to work with new arrivals, BME children and children with EAL, so they were strongly supported.

Commentary

The initial aim came from the perceived needs of the children in the class rather than curriculum content. It was connected to the local community and causes for concern in wider society.

 Individual or group activity

What values do you think are inherent in this proposed plan?

If you had identified these needs how would you progress in planning the actual learning outcomes and activities?

CASE STUDY 1 (CONTINUED)

Autumn term

The initial activity for the project explored 'Where am I connected to?' The children stood around a giant floor map of the world. They had coloured stickers and put these in places where they felt they had strong connections. They described what those were. For some it was where they themselves had been born and had lived, for others where their parents or grandparents originated; some had relatives living elsewhere in the world or had travelled on a memorable holiday.

They then looked at how long their families had lived in the local area. The children were asked to research and compile their family history. They devised questions to ask relatives they were in contact with, particularly looking at reasons for moving if they had moved (and there was much useful work on open and closed questions). The teachers were careful to support children who might find this activity emotionally difficult (for example those in foster care, those with only one parent they were in contact with or those who had arrived as refugees), but were also careful to value the experiences of children whose family had always lived in the area.

An early session helped the children prepare a list of activities they needed to do to achieve this task, to organise them in chronological order and make a checklist to monitor their progress. They also identified which tasks were likely to prove difficult and planned possible ways they could manage those difficulties.

This family history work continued into the second half of the term with interviews, collecting memorabilia, and writing up accounts. Some children managed to phone grandparents abroad to interview them; some received wonderful letters about their relatives' early lives. Children found out about how their parents had met, that they had had a life before their children arrived, and some families got very involved themselves through helping their children. The children took enormous care with their work and either made their own books or produced personalised folders to display their family history work, including photocopies of documents, maps and photographs.

Commentary

This section involved opportunities for the children to learn creatively by being given the chance to devise some of their own learning experiences. It was up to them to decide whom to contact and how that contact should be made, devise the list of questions they wanted to ask, and decide how to record that information. They were given both whole class and individual support with doing this.

The learning areas were in history and PSHE. The children had previously learned skills in historical enquiry based on particular National Curriculum study units, and they now used those skills independently, using oral testimony, pictures and documents to answer historical questions. This was set within a context that had real relevance to the children and their lives. This together with the links and connections with PSHE and flexible teaching methods produced a creative teaching experience.

The children were applying knowledge and skills learned previously to this task and the outcomes were decided personally. Each child decided how to communicate their findings in ways that suited them. There was ongoing evaluation of the task which informed subsequent activities, and they learned to undertake a long-term piece of work with persistence and determination, planning to meet interim goals on their way to the final outcome.

CASE STUDY 1 (CONTINUED)

Autumn/Spring term

In geography in the Autumn term the children studied the nature of their local area in relation to building a picture of the area of South London they lived in. This built on work they had done on the local area in previous years but linked it with the impressions of South London that their relatives had had in their childhood or when they first arrived in the area. The initial impressions of children who had recently arrived in the area were considered too. Key questions were: 'What is this place like? How has it changed?'

In the Spring term the focus moved to West Africa, with a history study unit on Ancient Benin and geography focusing on Nigeria and Ghana where many of the children's families had originated. (This work was undertaken prior to Year 6 starting the new National Curriculum in 2015.) They studied Benin City in modern Nigeria using photographs, maps of various types, video and written accounts to build up a picture of the area.

The class looked in some detail at fabric designs and explored the colours, textures and motifs using techniques with oil pastels to recreate various effects. They also explored the symbolism of animals in Ancient Benin and their stylised forms in modern West African design and the use of Ghanaian Adinkra symbols. A PSHE lesson asked each child to explore their personality, their hobbies and lifestyle, and then express these in visual symbolism. These were used to create an individual fabric panel in batik which summed up their essence and personality and these were joined together to make a class banner.

As part of the history of Ancient Benin the children came to know the story of Olaudah Equiano. This was used in English for work on biography and autobiography. Equiano wrote his own autobiography and the children looked at a short portion (it is quite dense eighteenth-century writing). They also looked in more depth at other autobiographical writing (Roald Dahl's *Boy* and Floella Benjamin's *Coming to England*) and used what they had learned about good descriptive language, tense and voice, and the differences between autobiography and biography, both to adapt autobiography into biography and to begin writing their own autobiographies. They took great pride in this writing and were able to explore lots of different stylistic devices through English lessons which they incorporated into their writing.

The autobiographies continued their stories, begun in their family histories, to the present day. As they were now approaching the end of their time at primary school, they enjoyed looking back at their journey and there was discussion about what they had learned, what had been their most memorable experiences, and what strengths and skills they now had.

Commentary

These activities are, of themselves, very unremarkable. However, the way they were linked and the way they built on the previous term's learning made for a depth of experience which resulted in remarkable children's learning. In terms of creativity there was again an emphasis on learning creatively in the personalised outcomes of the writing and art work and the discussions of their own 'learning journey' over their lives so far.

The teaching made links and connections between subjects and often had parallel learning objectives in two subjects. Time was often used flexibly, with work in English, linking closely with humanities subjects, being frequently time-tabled together.

The activities that led to designing and creating the batik panels involved generating new ideas in terms of the symbols they chose or making new meaning from traditional symbolism from other cultures. All the key criteria for working creatively were demonstrated in this activity.

CASE STUDY 1 (CONTINUED)

Summer term

In the Summer term the focus shifted to the question 'What is my culture?' This is a difficult concept so was started in a relatively simple way with investigating food. The children looked at their favourite foods and where they came from. They discussed foods that were eaten at family or religious celebrations and whether these were similar to or different from their chosen favourites. It was established that the foods the children particularly liked had originated from around the world and had often been brought here and established by people immigrating into the country. So their South London favourites – pizza, fried chicken, rice and peas, Chinese, kebabs etc. – reflected the various peoples who had settled in London over the years. Tastings of different foods and fruits were used to stimulate descriptive words which led into poetry about different foods. Parents were invited in to lead the cooking element of the class's D&T work. For example, after cooking Jollof rice the children investigated other West African foodstuffs that could be combined with rice in different ways and created their own dishes.

In a similar way the class traced the movement of stories and music. Using the story of Olaudah Equiano again, the children re-considered the slave triangle and diaspora (which they had explored in a previous year through story and drama) and also traced how elements of story and music had travelled across continents and been assimilated. For example, they traced certain creation myths and Anansi stories as well as call and response songs. As part of this work the class were fortunate enough to work with an African drumming group and a Caribbean dance group for workshops. They listened to lots of different instrumental, vocal, folk and pop music and tried to identify elements of the 'fusion' of different styles. At

(Continued)

(Continued)

each stage children from different ethnic groups were encouraged to use examples from their own culture and heritage. Much of the introduction of the stories and music was necessarily didactic. The children needed to identify different elements and be able to recognise these in different contexts. However, after the strong teacher input, and led by good questioning, they were able to make generalisations and apply their knowledge to new situations, including composing their own 'fusion' music.

Towards the end of term the children devised and designed an Identity Poster to sum up their work on the project. On one side was a selection of the children's poetry, illustrated by them. On the other side they identified the elements of what made up their identity in a rainbow diagram moving out from the centre, where individual self-portraits painted as miniatures in very delicate water colours were placed. Radiating out from these were also phrases they had written about the importance of identity.

The poster was designed to fold into an A5-size leaflet with a front and back cover. Its production provided a worthwhile enterprise project with the necessity for costing, design, fundraising and marketing activities. The children approached the school governors to apply for funding to print the poster and it was sold, at a price to cover costs, to parents and friends of the school.

As a culmination of the project the children made 'life braids'. They were given three lengths of ribbon. On one they wrote words that evoked their ancestry and cultural heritage, on another they wrote about themselves in the present, and on the third their hopes and dreams for the future. They plaited these to make their life braids which were hung up in the classroom. The children were enormously attached to their life braids, and at the end of term took them, their batik panel from the banner, their autobiography and family history, and all the other lovely things they had created which summed up their eleven years so far, and pointed them towards their future.

 ## Individual or group activity

Looking at the Summer term section of Case study 1 above, make your own commentary on the elements of creative learning and creative teaching you can identify in these activities. Which key elements of creativity would the children be able to exemplify and which skills in creativity would they need to use?

Using the Questions for Curriculum Planning (Chapter 8), how would the teacher involved have answered these questions? Are there any areas you think might have been missing? (From such a brief case study it is obviously difficult to ascertain all that was involved.)

What advantages and potential drawbacks do you see to this planning? (Bear in mind that subjects such as science, maths and PE were being taught discretely.)

CASE STUDY 2

The Quest

This case study is of a half-term's planning for a mixed-age class of 6 and 7 year olds (Years 1 and 2). The intention was to provide an engaging context for learning in geography and English using drama as the link and continuity.

In the first lesson when the children came into the classroom they found a mysterious letter. The teacher and children opened it together and the teacher read it out. The letter said:

Dear Children,

I wonder if you can help me? My people are in great trouble. We need your help.

If you will help me you will need to go on a mission. You will need to train hard for the mission. You will need to be brave and strong and clever.

Please let me know if you will help by leaving a letter for me in your classroom tonight.

I do hope you will. Your friend,

Salazar

P.S. If you will help, your first training is to learn how a map works.

The teacher led a discussion about who Salazar might be, what trouble he and his people might be in, whether the class felt they had the skills and temperament to go on the mission, and whether they wanted to help.

The class were enthusiastic about wanting to offer their help and the teacher organised a collaborative letter-writing activity to compose a letter to Salazar.

In the next session the teacher asked the children to remember what Salazar had asked them to do as training. They discussed what they knew about maps and shared some different types of maps – of countries, towns, road maps, street maps, and a map of the locality. The interactive whiteboard (IWB) was used to compare an aerial photograph of the school and surroundings with a map of the same view. As the mixed-age class were of widely different abilities there followed a variety of activities, including building a model town with building bricks, photographing it from above, and using the picture to draw a map.

In subsequent sessions children made their own maps of a route they knew well, and some children colour-coded and invented symbols for features such as roads, parkland, shops, bus stops, pillar boxes etc. Children gave instructions as to how to get to places around the school and school grounds, and other

(Continued)

(Continued)

children followed those instructions. The children eagerly anticipated a reply from Salazar and spent time looking at globes and maps at a variety of scales in their reading area, finding places, creating routes and discussing.

Commentary

The fiction of the letter asking for help sets the subsequent learning in an engaging context. The children wanted to do their best to learn about maps to be useful on their proposed mission. There was considerable interest from the class in looking at maps and they brought examples from home. Activities in the classroom allowed for individual interpretation in terms of creating their own choice of maps, symbols, keys etc.

CASE STUDY 2 (CONTINUED)

Once enough work had been done on learning about maps, the children came in one day to find there had been another letter. It congratulated them on learning about maps and asked them to find out about travelling through different environments and terrain.

This led to work building a geographical vocabulary and a knowledge and understanding of different types of terrain. The children looked at pictures of Arctic, desert and rainforest environments, cliffs, mountains and marshland etc. They also looked at video clips of similar environments. They discussed the features of the various environments. What is the weather like? What grows there? Which animals live there? What dangers would be there? How could you travel through this area?

They went to the hall and the children were asked to imagine they had to travel through these environments. Each environment was taken in turn and the children and teacher went for an imaginary walk, practising how to move, how hot or cold they were, pointing out features or animals, finding their way. Back in the classroom this led to generating good descriptive words and phrases which the children then used in individual descriptions of their chosen favourite environment. They also worked on different art techniques and colour mixing to paint or use collage to depict their environment.

The children then received another letter. This one congratulated them on being close to being ready for the final part of their quest. They were told they needed to show that they could follow a route on a map and a map of an imaginary place accompanied the letter. This large-scale map showed features such as a bridge, forest, river, roads, houses etc. The children discussed what the symbols on the map might mean and made a key at the bottom. They were then asked to plan a route from one point on the map to another, which they marked with arrows. The children were asked to describe what they would see as they followed that route. After doing this together as a group, pairs of children were given their own photocopied map and asked to mark and describe a route to each other, or individually to write a description of the route taken.

Commentary

The ability to visualise what a place looks like from a map is quite an advanced skill. That these young children were able to do this shows that their learning had depth and relevance. The teacher modelled activities so the children were confident when they attempted them individually. The teacher was able to move from their role as the skilled professional to a member of the quest team seamlessly. As a team member, the teacher's questions such as 'What do you think we should do now?' 'How could we get across there?' 'What should we take with us?' gave the children the chance to initiate ideas while giving the activities focus and purpose and maintaining the teacher's control of behaviour.

CASE STUDY 2 (CONTINUED)

The children received another letter telling them they were now ready for the final stage of their quest. They were told they had to go on a journey, following a map that was included with the letter, which would lead them to a place where something was hidden. They must find this and follow the instructions that were with it.

The children discussed the types of terrain that the map depicted and the route they would have to take. They went to the hall where drama blocks, benches etc. were set up to make obstacles to go over, under, along or round. The teacher and children began their imaginary journey, using the map, discussing the terrain they were covering, helping each other along ledges and across marshland, around swamps and through deserts. The teacher kept reinforcing the imaginary context with comments like, 'We've got to climb up to the bridge. Be careful, it's very wobbly. One at a time. Can you see the water down below?' The children finally found themselves at the site of a 'cave' (under a climbing frame draped with a curtain). Inside was a casket and a letter. Sitting down to rest they found the casket was full of tree seeds – conkers, sycamore, acorns and fruit pips – and the letter explained that a terrible storm had destroyed all the trees in Salazar's homeland. Only these few seeds were saved. Would the children take them and

(Continued)

(Continued)

find out how to plant them and nurture them so that the seedlings could be planted in Salazar's homeland?

The children returned to the classroom for a final discussion. They talked about how they felt having completed the quest. They reflected on the learning they had had to do to complete their task, and the stages of training and practising that had led them through it and why they had needed these. They also looked forward to the next half-term and what they would need to do to help Salazar plant new trees.

 ## Individual or group activities

What do you think the children learned during this sequence of lessons? How might their learning have been different if the lessons had not been within this imaginary context?

What skills did the teacher need to plan and teach this sequence of lessons?

What does this style of teaching and learning say about the classroom ethos?

Which aspects of creativity were missing from this unit of work that you might want to develop in the future?

The end of the quest set up the next half-term's science topic on how plants grow and the conditions they need to grow well. How would you plan that half-term? What would you want the children to gain in terms of knowledge, concepts, skills and values? Which subjects would you include and which would remain discrete? Could you concentrate on any of the aspects of creativity that you deemed to be missing or under-developed in the previous half-term?

Both the previous case studies were for extended periods of planning. The next example is for a single session, though it lasted for a whole morning.

CASE STUDY 3

The Shoe Shop

Background

This session took place as part of a school's Maths Week. Different activities were planned across the week, including inviting in adults to describe how they used maths in their work and daily lives, inviting parents to play maths games with their children and special activities that used maths in different contexts.

This half-day session involved 30 children aged from 7 to 9 (a mixed group from Years 2, 3 and 4).

The session took place in a hall with a few tables and chairs but plenty of floor space. Materials and resources were ready round the hall, although other resources could be brought from the nearby classroom if needed.

The Opening

The children and teacher sat in a circle on the floor. The teacher said, 'I'm going to tell you a story and I want you to help me tell it.'

The teacher knelt up.

Teacher: This story starts when my aunt was about to open a shoe shop. It wasn't just going to sell shoes it was going to repair them too. But just when the shop was nearly ready to open and all the posters and leaflets had gone out telling people when the grand opening was going to be, my aunt had to go into hospital. As you can imagine she was really upset and worried about what would happen to the shop because there was still lots of work to do, so obviously I offered to help. First I went down to the shop. My aunt said that she'd left a key with a neighbour so I went and knocked on her door.

[The teacher stood up and walked across the circle to stand in front of a child who she was sure would participate willingly. The teacher mimed knocking on the door.]

Teacher: Oh, hello. I think my aunt left the key to her shop with you. Have you got it?

Child: Oh, yes. Here it is.

Teacher: Could you come in with me?

[The teacher and child mimed opening the shop. They could not find the light and called on another child to help find the light switch and another to turn the electricity on. The teacher noticed a large pile of shoes outside the circle.]

Teacher: Oh, look at all these. Could you possibly sort them into pairs? Perhaps these neighbours who have dropped by could help you?

[Three more children from around the circle were drawn in to start sorting the shoes. The teacher continued to 'discover' jobs that needed to be done and

(Continued)

(Continued)

allocated children around the circle who were identified as helpful neighbours to do different activities.]

> Teacher: Oh, how wonderful that so many of you have offered to help. My aunt will be so pleased. You are so kind.

Soon all the children were involved in tasks. These included the following:

- Measuring laces and working out which length laces were needed for the different types of shoes. Then using a pre-prepared price list to work out how much it would cost to order ten of each of the required laces.
- Leather for making new soles was sold in square sheets 50cm wide. Using squared paper the children worked out how much leather an average pair of men's shoes would take. What about an average pair of women's shoes? If they mended five pairs of shoes each a week how much leather would they need to order?
- What were people's favourite colour shoes? Was it different for men, women and children? Did they prefer lace-ups or tape fastenings, slip-ons or straps? How could the children collect this information and use it to order more stock?
- Lots of the shoes had come without boxes. Could the children design and make shoeboxes for different-sized shoes?
- Tiny nails were needed to mend some boots. These were sold by weight. If nails were placed every centimetre around a sole how many were needed for each pair? How much did these weigh? What weight of nails should they order to have enough for mending 20 pairs? Or 50 pairs?

Once all the children were involved in tasks the teacher circulated asking questions to help them define their task or find other ways of solving their problem. Additional activities were added where children needed extension and lots of 'What if … ?' questions were asked.

At this stage the children were all involved in investigative activities and had probably largely forgotten about the 'story' they were in. Towards the end of the session they were called together. The teacher asked each group what they had achieved and what they thought still needed to be done. Then the teacher rounded up the session.

> Teacher: So, everyone worked really hard to help the shop be ready. My aunt came out of hospital just in time for the opening and was amazed and so pleased at what her friends and neighbours had done to help. Everyone was invited to the grand opening and a big party to say thank you and the shop was a great success.

Individual or group activity

This was a one-off special session – what value does this type of activity have? What are the drawbacks?

What potential would there be to include this type of activity in day-to-day teaching and learning?

What elements of creativity were evident in this session? What were the necessary prerequisites for the children to be able to participate in this activity fully and get the most out of it?

How would you plan to follow this activity up if that were possible?

Commentary on all the case studies

These three case studies show different aspects of creativity. The first is the most extensive, with a theme that lasts over the course of the whole year, and most curriculum subjects are linked to it at some stage in the year, although not all at once. This is a complex piece of planning but shows how the children's social and emotional needs as well as their learning needs can influence choices in planning. It also shows how elements of the National Curriculum can be given cohesion and relevance by the way they are combined and the context they are placed in. The children in this case study were able to apply skills and knowledge learned in previous years to personalised and individual pieces of work that were often extensive.

The second case study used an imaginative setting to give relevance and build motivation. It combined fewer curriculum subjects than the first case study and was of shorter duration, but provided a rich context within which the learning could happen. As team members on the quest the children were given opportunities to show leadership and responsibility and in their writing and art work to make personal choices about how to apply their learning.

The third case study only involved one subject and one session but gave the children opportunities for open-ended investigative working, and the imaginative setting simulated a 'real life' situation that motivated them to engage deeply with their learning.

It is unlikely that any unit of work will 'tick all the boxes' that we have identified for different types of creativity. It will be important to keep track via assessment of children's learning and reflection on and evaluation of our own planning and teaching, and so be able to plan subsequent activities that allow for progression and learning in different areas. It is important to analyse exactly which elements of creativity are being addressed. It is far better to plan an occasional lesson that gives children the chance to investigate and explore open-ended questions, than to try to link everything to a 'theme' and end up with tenuous links and uninspiring activities.

Starting small and building up gradually are always a good idea. Use the planning checklists in Chapters 7 and 8 to identify retrospectively elements you have addressed in lessons you have taught, and then choose one or two elements you have not yet used to focus on next time. As these techniques are used, refined and repeated they will become part of your teaching 'repertoire', and teaching creatively and fostering creativity in the children you teach will become second nature.

 Further study

Critical reflection: Activity 9

Allow an hour for this activity.

Synthesise the learning that you take from Chapters 7, 8 and 9.

In the Further Study section in Chapter 7 you identified a subject you wished to teach more creatively. *Examine* the subject knowledge, skills, concepts and learning styles this subject involves. *Compare and contrast* these with other curriculum subjects and *look for commonalities, differences and interrelationships.*

Identify opportunities for fruitful links and connections between two or three of these subjects. Plan a short sequence of lessons using these connections. *Identify* the key elements of creativity that the children will be developing. *Recognise* the values inherent in this sequence.

Use the Forward Planning section in the Conclusion to *identify* how you are going to continue to grow in creativity and being a creative teacher who encourages children's creativity to develop. Plan the next steps you will take.

Identify how and when you will monitor and evaluate your progress. What will help you to keep to this?

Consider the implications of continuing to develop your planning and teaching in this way. What benefits and/or drawbacks do you foresee? *Identify* how you will plan to mitigate the drawbacks and promote the benefits.

 Further reading

Grainger, T., Barnes, J. and Scoffham, S. (2006) 'Creativity for Tomorrow'. Research report for Creative Partnerships. Margate: Creative Partnerships.

Jeffrey, B. (ed.) (2006) *Creative Learning Practices: European Experiences.* London: Tufnell.

Woods, P. and Jeffrey, B. (1996) *Teachable Moments: The Art of Creative Teaching in Primary Schools.* Buckingham: Open University Press.

CONCLUSION AND FORWARD PLANNING

The intention of this book was to give an insight into the different facets of creativity in the primary school classroom – the children's growing creativity, the teacher's use of creative activities and planning, and the application of the key elements of creativity into teaching and learning in different subjects. Hopefully it has also stimulated a desire to be a more creative teacher and to create learning environments and situations for children where they can be creative and develop their own creativity. Making this happen in practice will require more than just having read this book; the following section gives some guidance as to how to proceed and forward plan to make those changes in your practice.

Making changes in any area of life involves many different stages and a degree of concentrated effort. It does not just happen because you want it to. It mirrors the learning that we are encouraging the children in our classrooms to undertake, with all the necessity for repetition, resilience, persistence, reflection, determination and an ability to set targets and work towards them. As such it can be a salutary example of the personal and learning skills we ask children to use every day.

As has already been stated, the most effective way to increase the creativity in your classroom is to do it in small steps. Having a plan of the stages you will need to go through and regularly reflecting on your progress and updating the plan are undoubtedly the best way forward.

Formulating the plan

1. Consider the way the children are used to learning at the present time – the classroom environment, both physical and in terms of ethos, and the way you generally plan and teach. Identify one goal you would like to achieve in each of these three areas.
2. Think about each goal in turn. Does it need breaking down into smaller stages? If so, do this now. Plan the activities you will undertake to achieve your goals.
3. Do you need to undertake any more research about the goals you have in mind? Perhaps this might involve looking back in this book to where the idea was introduced, doing some further reading, or observing the technique in action in a classroom.
4. How will you know whether you have been successful in the challenges you have set yourself? What are the success criteria you will be looking for?
5. What constraints might there be to the success of the changes you are planning to make? Identify possible hindrances and plan ways you will deal with these if they occur.
6. Set a timescale to achieve these goals. Be realistic – you may not be able to do all three at once and might need to space these out. Set a time when you will evaluate your progress; this might be as part of your regular weekly evaluation or a particular date you set for yourself.

Reflection, evaluation and forward planning

At the time you set aside to consider your progress ask yourself the following questions:

- Did I achieve what I had planned? How do I know? What benefits has this produced?
- If I did not achieve or only partially achieved my goal why was that? Can I remedy the situation? Should I change my plan?
- What next steps will I take? (Repeat the process above.)

Congratulate yourself for what you have achieved. Even if you did not achieve what you set out to do, you will have learned some valuable lessons about yourself, the school and class you are in, your expectations and what is possible. These will be invaluable as you plan what to do next.

Next steps

As you pursue the route to becoming a more creative teacher you will move further away from what you remember reading in this book. The journey is likely to be a long one, probably one that lasts a whole career. As part of your reflective journey, try to return to the activities in this book from time to time. It may be that you skimmed through some of the activities and did not actually carry them out in detail as you went. If so, try to make time to address the activities in some depth, perhaps collaborating when applicable with a colleague to discuss, compare and share notes. Learning is likely to be deeper and more readily used if you have applied it in different contexts.

Make time when you can to read further around the subject and observe and question what you see in classrooms. If you did not use the Further Study activities first time round come back to these and use them. They will help extend reflection into action and make that reflection more critical and more scholarly.

Final thoughts

You will have understood through the chapters of this book that creativity is not an easy option, that it involves rigour and an active reflective process. It is not the only way of learning, however. It can provide stimulus and extension, experimentation, enquiry and expression, but needs to be integrated with all the other ways of acquiring information, knowledge and skills to use in a variety of contexts.

In the classroom you will be assessing the learning of the children in regular formative and summative ways. These and your ongoing reflections will tell you if the creative approaches you use, and the encouragement of creativity in the children you teach, are having an effect on their learning and their attitudes to learning. There will be other benefits as well, as the following quotes from teachers who have experienced learning in creative contexts show:

'The buzz in the room was incredible. They loved the freedom. Their group work skills have increased greatly. It's become part of how they work, they are really thinking. Their social skills have developed really well too.' (Teacher)

'I have begun to "let go" a little and have the kids leading the process rather than always being teacher-led. It has been great to see how much more they get out of the work and how it inspires everyone in the class.' (Teacher)

Creative approaches inspire children to learn, and developing their own creativity opens up a world of opportunities in work, leisure and relationships that will last a lifetime. Start small and build up gradually, and enjoy the depth of learning and the revelations and insights of the creative child.

Good luck!

REFERENCES

Books and articles

Abbs, P. (2003) *Against the Flow*. London: Routledge.

Adams, P. (1992) *Mrs Honey's Hat*. Swindon: Child's Play.

Ahlberg, A. and Ahlberg, J. (1999) *Each Peach Pear Plum*. London: Puffin.

Alexander, R. (ed.) (2010) *Children, Their World, Their Education: The Report of the Cambridge Primary Review*. London: Routledge.

Arthur, J. and Cremin, T. (eds) (2010) *Learning to Teach in the Primary School*, 2nd edn. London: Routledge.

Baldwin, P. (2008) *The Primary Drama Handbook: An Introduction*. London: Sage.

Bannerman, C. (2008) 'Creativity and wisdom', in A. Craft, H. Gardner and G. Claxton (eds), *Creativity, Wisdom and Trusteeship: Exploring the Role of Education*. Thousand Oaks, CA: Corwin Press, pp. 133–42.

Barnes, J. (2015) *Cross-Curricular Learning 3–14*, 2nd edn. London: Sage.

Belbin, R.M. (1981) *Management Teams: Why They Succeed or Fail*, 3rd edn. Oxford: Elsevier.

Bloom, B., Englehart, M., Furst, E., Hill, W. and Krathwohl, D. (1956) *Taxonomy of Educational Objectives: The Classification of Educational Goals. Handbook 1: Cognitive Domain*. New York: David McKay.

Boden, M. (2001) 'Creativity and knowledge', in A. Craft, B. Jeffrey and M. Leibling (eds), *Creativity in Education*. London: Continuum, pp. 95–102.

Browne, E. (1994) *Handa's Surprise*. London: Walker.

Central Advisory Council for Education (Plowden Report) (1967) *Children and Their Primary Schools*. London: HMSO.

Claxton, G. (2002) *Building Learning Power*. London: TLO.

Craft, A. (2000) *Creativity across the Primary Curriculum*. London: Routledge.

Craft, A. (2005) *Creativity in Schools: Tensions and Dilemmas*. London: Routledge.

Craft, A., Gardner, H. and Claxton, G. (eds) (2008) *Creativity, Wisdom and Trusteeship: Exploring the Role of Education*. Thousand Oaks, CA: Corwin Press.

Craft, A., Jeffrey, B. and Leibling, M. (eds) (2001) *Creativity in Education*. London: Continuum.

Csikszentmihalyi, M. (1990) *Flow: The Psychology of Optimal Experience*. New York: HarperPerennial.

Csikszentmihalyi, M. (1996) *Creativity, Flow and the Psychology of Discovery and Invention*. New York: Harper Collins.

DCMS/DfES (Department for Culture, Media and Sport/Department for Education and Skills) (2006) *Nurturing Creativity in Young People: A Report to Government to inform Future Policy*. London: DfES.

de Bono, E. (1999) *Six Thinking Hats*. London: Penguin.

DfE (Department for Education) (2010) *The Importance of Teaching*. The Schools White Paper. London: TSO.

DfE (Department for Education) (2011) *Review of the National Curriculum in England: Remit*. London: DfE.

DfE (Department for Education) (2014) *The National Curriculum in England Framework Document*. London: DfE.

DfEE/QCA (Department for Education and Employment/Qualification and Curriculum Authority) (1999) *The National Curriculum: Handbook for Primary Teachers in England: Key Stages 1 and 2*. London: DfEE.

DfES (Department for Education and Skills) (2003) *Excellence and Enjoyment: A Strategy for Primary Schools*. Nottingham: DfES.

DfES (Department for Education and Skills) (2004) *Excellence and Enjoyment: Learning and Teaching in the Primary Years*. Nottingham: DfES.

DfES (Department for Education and Skills) (2005) *Excellence and Enjoyment: Social and Emotional Aspects of Learning*. Nottingham: DfES.

Edwards, C. et al. (eds) (1993) *The Hundred Languages of Children: The Reggio Emilia Approach to Early Childhood Education*. New York: Ablex.

Fisher, R. (2006) 'Thinking skills', in J. Arthur, T. Grainger and D. Wray (eds), *Learning to Teach in Primary School*. London: RoutledgeFalmer.

Fleming, M. (2011) *Starting Drama Teaching*, 3rd edn. London: David Fulton.

Gardner, H. (1993) *Multiple Intelligences: The Theory in Practice*. New York: Basic Books.

Gillard, D. (2011) *The History of Education in England*. Available at www.educationengland/org.uk (last accessed 13 July 2011).

Glazzard, J., Hughes, A., Netherwood, A., Neve, L. and Stokoe, J. (2010) *Teaching Primary Special Educational Needs*. London: Sage.

Goleman, D. (1996) *Emotional Intelligence*. London: Bloomsbury.

Hattie, J. (2009) *Visible Learning*. London: Routledge.

Hirsch, E.D. (1996) *The Schools We Need and Why We Don't Have Them*. New York: Doubleday.

HMI (2003) *Expecting the Unexpected – Developing Creativity in Primary and Secondary Schools*. HMI 1612. London: Ofsted.

Horowitz, A. (2000) *Stormbreaker*. London: Walker.

Hughes, S. (1997) *Dogger*. London: Red Fox.

Hutchins, P. (1998) *Rosie's Walk*. London: Bodley Head.

Jeffrey, B. and Craft, A. (2001) 'The universalization of creativity in education', in A. Craft, B. Jeffrey and M. Leibling (eds), *Creativity in Education*. London: Continuum, pp. 1–14.

Jeffrey, B. and Craft, A. (2004) 'Teaching creatively and teaching for creativity: distinctions and relationships', *Educational Studies*, 30 (1): 77–8.

Joubert, M.M. (2001) 'The art of creative teaching: NACCCE and beyond', in A. Craft, B. Jeffrey and M. Leibling (eds), *Creativity in Education*. London: Chapman.

Lave, J. and Wenger, E. (1991) *Situated Learning*. Cambridge: Cambridge University Press.

Leahy, S. and Wiliam, D. (2013) *Embedding formative assessment professional development* (3rd edn). CD Rom. SSAT (The Schools Network).

Lipman, M., Sharp, A.M. and Oscanyan, F.S. (1980) *Philosophy in the Classroom*, 2nd edn. Philadelphia, PA: Temple University Press.

Lucas, B. (2001) 'Creative teaching, teaching creativity and creative learning', in A. Craft, B. Jeffrey and M. Leibling (eds), *Creativity in Education*. London: Continuum, pp. 35–44.

Luff, P. (2013) 'Play and creativity', in T. Waller and G. Davis (eds), *An Introduction to Early Childhood,* 3rd edn. London: Sage, Chapter 7.

McFall, M. (2013) *The Little Book of Awe and Wonder: A Cabinet of Curiosities*. Carmarthen: Independent Thinking Press (an imprint of Crown House Publishing).

McGuinness, C. (1999) *From Thinking Skills to Thinking Classrooms: A Review and Evaluation of Approaches for Developing Pupils' Thinking*. Research Report RR15. London: DfEE.

NACCCE (National Advisory Committee on Creative and Cultural Education) (1999) *All Our Futures: Creativity, Culture and Education*. London: DfEE.

OECD (Organisation for Economic Cooperation and Development) (2011) *Strong Performers and Successful Reformers in Education: Lessons from PISA for the United States*. Paris: OECD Publishing. Available at http://dx.doi.org/10.1787/9789264096660-en

Ofsted (2010) *Learning: Creative Approaches that Raise Standards*. London: Ofsted.

Phillips, R. (2004) *Numbers: Facts, Figures and Fiction,* 2nd edn. Evesham: Badsey.

PWC (Price Waterhouse-Coopers) (2001) *Teacher Workload Study*. London: DfES.

QCA (Qualifications and Curriculum Authority) (2005) *Creativity: Find it, Promote it.* London: QCA.

Reynolds, D. (1998) 'Schooling for literacy: a review of research on teacher effectiveness and school effectiveness and its implications for contemporary educational policy', *Educational Review*, 50 (2): 147–62.

Reynolds, D. and Muijs, D. (1999) 'The effective teaching of mathematics: a review of research', *School Leadership and Management*, 19 (3): 273–88.

Robinson, K. (2001) *Out of Our Minds.* Oxford: Capstone.

Rogers, B. (2006) *Classroom Behaviour: A Practical Guide to Effective Behaviour Management and Colleague Support.* London: Paul Chapman.

Rose, J. (2009) *Independent Review of the Primary Curriculum.* London: DCSF.

Rudduck, J. (2005) 'Pupil voice is here to stay!', *QCA Futures – Meeting the Challenge.* London: QCA Online.

Safran, L. (2001) 'Creativity as "mindful" learning', in A. Craft, B. Jeffrey and M. Leibling (eds), *Creativity in Education.* London: Continuum, pp. 80–92.

Sawyer, R.K. (2012) *Explaining Creativity: The Science of Human Innovation,* 2nd edn. New York: Oxford University Press.

Schwartz, R.M. (2002) *The Skilled Facilitator: A Comprehensive Resource for Consultants, Facilitators, Managers and Coaches.* San Francisco, CA: Jossey-Bass.

Shelton, F. and Brownhill, S. (2008) *Effective Behaviour Management in the Primary Classroom.* Maidenhead: Open University Press.

Smithers, A. and Robinson, P. (2001) *Teachers Leaving.* Centre for Education and Employment Research. London: NUT.

Stein, M. (1974) *Stimulating Creativity*, Vol. 1. New York: Academic Press.

Torrance, E.P. (1965) *Rewarding Creative Behaviour.* Englewood Cliffs, NJ: Prentice-Hall.

Wragg, E.C. and Brown, G. (2001) *Questioning.* London: Routledge.

Wray, D. (2010) 'Looking at learning', in J. Arthur and T. Cremin (eds), *Learning to Teach in the Primary School*, 2nd edn. London: Routledge, pp. 53–65.

Websites

Access Art – Sketchbooks in schools (www.accessart.org.uk/tag/sketch books/). This website aims to promote, inspire and enable the creative use of sketchbooks in primary schools (last accessed January 2015).

Burton, I. (Nottingham City Music Service) and D'Amore, A., *Co-constructing a Curriculum* (www.musicalfutures.org.uk/resource/27349). An on-line teacher's resource by Part of Musical Futures. Link shows details of pupil co-construction (last accessed January 2015).

Creative Learning Journey (www.creativelearningjourney.org.uk). Website of primary curriculum organised around the six areas of learning from the Early Years Foundation Stage curriculum (last accessed January 2015).

Dalton, J. and Smith, D. (1986) *Extending Children's Special Abilities – Strategies for Primary Classrooms* (www.esc14.net/docs/18-ctl_bm_blooms_ cards_cubes_and_chart.pdf). This useful chart gives ideas for questions and activities based on Bloom's Taxonomy. Also designs for a cube and wallchart to use (last accessed January 2015).

Every Child Matters (www.education.gov.uk/consultations/downloadableDocs/ EveryChildMatters.pdf). The Every Child Matters document (last accessed January 2015).

Gillard, D. (2011) www.educationengland.org.uk/history. This website outlines the history of education in England over 1400 years. It includes links to the text of speeches, papers and legislation, and important educational theorists (last accessed January 2015).

SAPERE (Society for Advancing Philosophical Enquiry and Reflection in Education) www.sapere.org.uk. This educational charity promotes philosophical enquiry for children (often known as P4C) (last accessed January 2015).

Teaching and Learning Research Programme (2005) www.tlrp.org.uk. The Teaching and Learning Research Programme was the UKs largest-ever educational research programme. It coordinated some 700 researchers in over 100 projects. www.tlrp.org/pub/documents/ BlatchfordRBFinal_001.pdf is the link to the research briefing on the *Improving Pupil Group Work in Classrooms* project (last accessed January 2015).

UN Convention on the Rights of the Child (www.unicef.org.uk/Documents/ Publications/Child_friendly_CRC_summary_final.pdf). This link takes you to a poster on the rights of the child in child-friendly language (last accessed January 2015).

Questioning to promote learning: Ofsted 2012 (www.fromgoodtooutstanding. com/2012/05/ofsted-2012-questioning-to-promote-learning). This is part of the website *From good to outstanding: promoting outstanding, creative and enjoyable learning*. It includes video clips and examples (last accessed January 2015).

INDEX